Henry Wikoff

A letter to Viscount Palmerston, K.G.

prime minister of England, on American slavery

Henry Wikoff

A letter to Viscount Palmerston, K.G.
prime minister of England, on American slavery

ISBN/EAN: 9783744729291

Printed in Europe, USA, Canada, Australia, Japan

Cover: Foto ©ninafisch / pixelio.de

More available books at **www.hansebooks.com**

A

LETTER

TO

VISCOUNT PALMERSTON, K.G.,

PRIME MINISTER OF ENGLAND,

ON

AMERICAN SLAVERY.

BY

HENRY WIKOFF,

AUTHOR OF "A VISIT TO HAM," ETC., ETC.

———◆◆———

NEW YORK:

PUBLISHED BY ROSS & TOUSEY,

121 NASSAU STREET.

1861.

6.

RENNIE, SHEA & LINDSAY,
STEREOTYPERS AND ELECTROTYPERS,
81, 83 & 85 CENTRE-STREET,
NEW YORK

PREFACE.

THIS letter was originally intended for the private perusal of the Noble Lord to whom it is addressed; but it was suggested to me that its publication here might possibly be beneficial. In the hope, then, that it may be found in some degree interesting, if not useful, I do not hesitate to give it to the Public.

HENRY WIKOFF.

BREVOORT HOUSE,
New York, *January* 28, 1861.

"The science of government is merely a science of combinations, of applications, and of exceptions, according to time, place, and circumstances."—ROUSSEAU.

"The surest way to prevent seditions, if the times do bear it, is to take away the matter of them; for if there be fuel prepared, it is hard to tell whence the spark shall come that shall set it on fire."—LORD BACON.

"Power exercised with violence has seldom been of long duration, but temper and moderation generally produce permanence in all things."—SENECA.

TO

VISCOUNT PALMERSTON, K.G.,

&c., &c., &c.

———————◆•●———————

My Lord,

 Just ten years since, your Lordship was at the head of the
Foreign Office of England. A war of parties then raged in
France which threatened to end in anarchy. The interests of
England, so closely identified with France, required that every
phase of the conflict should be known to your Lordship. I was
at that moment a watchful but dispassionate observer of these
events, and had the honor to furnish your Lordship officially
with such information as my opportunities, somewhat rare,
enabled me to acquire.

 At the present hour, your Lordship occupies a still more illus-
trious post—the Premiership of England. A fierce contest of
sections has broken out in this country, which foreshadows
disruption and ruin. Again, the interests of England, still more
closely interwoven with the United States, demand that every
feature of this internecine strife should be familiar to your Lordship. A calm, but not unconcerned spectator of the turmoil, I
venture, though no longer a duty, to lay before your Lordship a
simple outline of this portentous crisis. It is all-important that
the government and people of England should understand it, in
order that the action of the one and the sentiments of the other
should be wisely guided and judiciously formed. The task is
onerous, and exacts higher capacity. A native of this country,*

---

* Born in Philadelphia, and a graduate of Yale College.

however, and familiar with its history and institutions, I am
not wholly disqualified. My knowledge of England will also
enable me to make intelligible what might otherwise be obscure, if, indeed, aught can elude the practical, searching analysis
common to your Lordship. My respect for the lofty position of
your Lordship, but still more for the intellect and character that
adorn it, will compel me to be scrupulous in my facts and impartial in my statements. With such data your Lordship will
apply the test to my conclusions.

Immersed in the politics of Europe, and for near half a century an occupant of office, your Lordship can only have glanced
at this country, so far removed, when a question of moment
required attention. Allow me, then, to pass in rapid review
its domestic political history, which will tend to elucidate the
present situation.

Political Review.

The movement that threw off the rule of the mother country,
began in the New England Colonies. These were settled by
those Puritans who effected the Revolution of 1620, and
decapitated Charles I. The Southern Colonies were occupied
by a more loyal class. To the noble family of Baltimore was
granted, by Royal Charter, the province of Maryland. To other
staunch adherents of the crown were accorded grants and
privileges in Virginia, North and South Carolina, and Georgia.

With antecedents so opposite, both North and South joined
heartily in the War of Independence, making equal sacrifices
and dividing fairly its triumphs. In 1781, the struggling States
formed a Confederation, and essayed self-government. The
first experiment failed, when the present Union was established.
The written Charter of 1789 followed the form and usages of
the British Constitution. Supreme power was divided between
the executive and legislative branches; but all were elective.
The executive power was vested in one person for a term of
four years, with special duties assigned. The Legislature was
divided, as in England, into two Houses, with separate prerog-

atives. All power not positively delegated to this Federal Government was reserved to the States. The problem of popular government was once more undertaken.

Gen. Washington was the first Federal magistrate, chosen from a list of twelve candidates.

Up to this period, the politicians of the country had, first, contended in a body against the supremacy of the mother country; and, next, had united their energies in the structure of a Republican Constitution.

During President Washington's term, they divided into two hostile parties, each striving for office through the profession of opposite principles. The New England States, led by John Adams, advocated the power of the Federal Government, even to straining the Constitution. This was the Federal party. The Southern States, led by Thomas Jefferson, maintained State rights against Federal encroachment. This was the Democratic party.

In 1797, John Adams, of Massachusetts, was elected* President of the Confederacy. During his term, the Alien† and Sedition‡ laws were passed by the Federal Congress. These enactments were opposed by the statesmen of the South, since, in their opinion, they invested the Executive with powers not conferred by the Constitution and inimical to popular rights. The creation of a National Bank was also a subject of keen controversy. The public men of the North sustained it with energy, while those of the South opposed it as unconstitutional and of doubtful expediency.

In 1801, Thomas Jefferson, of Virginia, was elected President. During this term the New England States displayed a bitter animosity to the South, which arose, chiefly, from the South having put a limit to the slave-trade, in which these

---

* The election for President takes place four months before his inauguration, but I shall use the words sinonymously.

† By the Alien law, June, 1800, the President might order all such aliens as he deemed dangerous to quit the country, on pain of three years' imprisonment and civil disability.

‡ By the Sedition law, any person who should libel the President, or either House of Congress, should be fined $2,000, and be imprisoned for two years.

States were profitably engaged. When, therefore, President Jefferson proposed the purchase of Louisiana from France, the Eastern States violently resisted, because it increased the territory and power of the South. Congress empowered the purchase, April, 1803.

In 1805, Thomas Jefferson was re-elected to the Presidency. His second term was troubled by the war between England and France. The Berlin and Milan Decrees of Napoleon, and the Orders in Council of the British Government, equally assailed American interests. Our vessels, bound either to English or French ports, incurred capture and confiscation. This left but one alternative, either to abandon our trade with Europe, or go to war to protect it. To escape the latter, President Jefferson recommended an Embargo Act, to put a temporary stop to all our foreign trade. This was vehemently opposed by the New England States, because their interests, being chiefly commercial, were seriously damaged. The Embargo Act was passed by Congress in December, 1807; whereupon the Eastern States threatened to secede from the Union, and form a Northern Confederacy.

In 1809, James Madison, of Virginia, was elected President. Soon after his accession, March, 1809, the Embargo Act was repealed, to appease the New England States; and a less stringent law, the Non-Intercourse Act, was passed by Congress, May, 1809, which prohibited trade with England and France. New England, however, carried on an indirect trade with Europe, through Canada. In spite of all these precautions by the Government, our interests and dignity were incessantly outraged by England. Finally, the indignation of the country compelled Congress to declare war, May, 1812.

In 1813, James Madison was re-elected President. During the war, the Government was supported by direct taxes and requisitions upon the States; but the New England States refused, for the most part, to contribute.* The war closed, January, 1815. To resuscitate the Federal treasury, a new financial policy was inaugurated. A Tariff of high duties was passed by

* Niles' Register.

Congress, April, 1816. New England advocated this law, because, during the war, she had transferred her capital from commerce to manufactures, for which she desired protection. The South was injured by the Tariff, but she supported it from patriotic motives. John C. Calhoun, of South Carolina, went so far as to introduce a *minimum* rate for *ad valorem* duties, that is, a rate below which the duties should not fall.* A new National Bank act was also passed, April, 1816; the old one having expired in 1811.

In 1817, James Monroe, of Virginia, was elected President. During this term the interests of the country prospered. No struggle occurred between the politicians of New England and the South till 1820, when Missouri applied for admission into the Union as a Slave State. The Eastern States opposed it violently, on the ground of extending slavery. The Union was in danger of dissolution, when, finally, Missouri was admitted by Congress as a Slave State, on the compromise that thereafter no Slave States should be created north of 36° 30' parallel of latitude.

In 1821, James Monroe was re-elected President. During this term, a new conflict arose between the politicians of New England and those of the South, on the subject of the Tariff policy inaugurated at the peace. New England demanded more protection for her manufactures. This the South opposed, on the ground that her manufactures had protection enough, and next, because an increase of the Tariff was seriously detrimental to the interests of the South.

In 1825, John Quincy Adams, of Massachusetts, was elected President.† During this term, a heated contest was carried on between New England and the South, on the Tariff policy. In 1828, a new act was passed by Congress, which raised the duties to an almost prohibitory standard. The average was 40 per cent. on imports. The South designated this act as the " Black Tariff."

---

* At the instance of Mr. Lowell, the father of manufactures in Massachusetts.

† This election was made by the House of Representatives, as provided in the Constitution, in default of an election by the people.

In 1829, Andrew Jackson, of Tennessee, became President. During this term, the extreme Tariff policy of New England led to violent remonstrance in South Carolina, whose interests were seriously injured. She alleged that a policy to enrich one section of the country at the expense of another, was unjust and unconstitutional. She threatened to resist this policy by force. A compromise was effected, March, 1833, by which the obnoxious Tariff was modified by Congress.

In 1833, Andrew Jackson was re-elected President. During this term, an acrimonious struggle was carried on between the politicians of the North* and South, on the National Bank created at the peace. The former maintained it was necessary to their trade and commerce: the latter, while denying its constitutionality and expediency, also avowed their fears of its becoming a political machine, that might, in the hands of unscrupulous politicians, do much harm. The charter was allowed to expire in 1836. A policy known under the name of "Internal Improvements," was also discussed in this term. It had the support of the North, but the South opposed it as favoring one section at the cost of the others.

In 1837, Martin Van Buren, of New York, was elected President. During this term, great financial disorder prevailed in the country. The Northern politicians proposed, as a panacea, a new National Bank, a higher Tariff, and a Bankrupt Law. The South opposed them all, as unnecessary and sectional in their tendency.

In 1841, William Henry Harrison, of Ohio, was elected President. He died soon after his accession to office. The Presidency was then administered by the Vice-president. John Tyler, of Virginia, as provided by the Constitution. During this term, Northern policy mostly prevailed. The Tariff was augmented, September, 1841, and August, 1842. A Bankrupt Law was passed, August, 1841.+ A law was carried through Congress, July, 1841, dividing the public domain among the

---

* The Northern Politicians dropped the title of "Federalist" in 1824, and assumed that of "Whig" in 1828.

+ By this act, private debts to the amount of 440 millions of dollars (88 millions sterling) were cancelled.

respective States, in proportion to their population. The effect of this was favorable to the manufacturing States of New England; for, by cutting off from the Federal treasury the receipts from the public lands, it made a higher Tariff imperative, to insure a sufficient revenue. The new bank charter failed. At the end of eighteen months, the Bankrupt Act was repealed, 1843. A new Slave State, Texas, was admitted to the Union, March 3, 1845. The act for dividing the public lands was repealed, January, 1842, as it was found necessary to retain them as security for Federal loans.

In 1845, James K. Polk, of Tennessee, was inaugurated President. During his term, the Tariff, which was pressing heavily on the interests of the South, was modified, July, 1846. The President, in a special message to Congress, May, 1846, announced that the Government of Mexico had committed an act of war against the Confederacy. On this occasion, all sections of the country, North and South and West, united in declaring war against Mexico. The war closed, February, 1848. The treaty of Guadalupe-Hidalgo, which followed, ceded California and New Mexico to the United States.

In 1849, Zachary Taylor, of Mississippi, became President. During this term, the old issues between the politicians of the North and South were abandoned, to wit: the Tariff policy, a National Bank, a system of Internal Improvements, a Division of the Public Lands. The recent acquisitions of territory, however, afforded the public men of both sections a fertile field of discussion. The North contended against admitting slavery into the new territory. The South declared that its right to joint occupation was incontestable, both in law and equity, and proposed that the compromise of 1820 should be renewed, by extending the Missouri line of 36° 30′ to the Pacific Ocean. This the politicians of the North refused. The controversy became so violent that a separation of the North and South seemed imminent. A compromise, however, took place in 1850, which stopped the discussion, but did not settle the main point in dispute, namely, the right of the South to joint occupation of all new territory.

In 1853, Franklin Pierce, of New Hampshire, became President. During this term, the discussion on slavery was unfortunately renewed. A portion of western territory, named
Nebraska,* was divided into two territories. One of these
was called Kansas, and the other Nebraska. The compromise
line of 36° 30′ ran to the south of these territories, which would
have given Kansas as well as Nebraska, the largest, to the North.
On the proposition of the senator from Illinois, Stephen A.
Douglas, the compromise line was repealed by Congress. An
effort was subsequently made by the South to occupy Kansas,
in order to make it a Slave State. This the North determined
to resist. Emigrant societies were established in Massachusetts
and Connecticut, in 1854, to furnish pecuniary aid to settlers in
Kansas. In consequence, a hostile population from North and
South poured into Kansas, whose interests and sentiments were
antagonistic and irreconcilable. Civil dissensions of great bitterness, at length, terminated in conflict. Bands of armed men
from the North and South paraded the territory, and frequently
came in collision, with loss of life. The Federal Government,
whose jurisdiction extended over this distant country, was
finally forced to interfere. The leaders of the anti-slavery
propaganda, having violated the Federal prerogative by passing
a constitution† and electing a governor, were indicted for
treason, and obliged to take to flight.‡

In 1857, James Buchanan, of Pennsylvania, was inaugurated
President. The whole of this term has been disturbed by a
heated contest between the politicians of the North and South,
on the subject of slavery in the territories. The civil troubles
in Kansas were renewed by the leaders of the pro-slavery party
drafting a constitution§ favorable to their views, which Congress refused to ratify. It follows that Kansas, though qualified by population to become a State, still remains a territory,

* 1,800 miles from Washington.
† Called the Topeka Constitution, after the village where the Convention met.
‡ The Northern Politicians, during this term, dropped the appellation of " Whig,"
and assumed that of " Republican," better known as " Black Republican."
§ Called the Lecompton Constitution, after the place where the Convention
assembled.

a prey to the sectional animosities that divide her. Towards the close of this Presidency, the prolonged strife between the politicians of the North and South on the topic of slavery, was taken up by the people of these respective sections, in an election for a new president, November, 1860. The Northern States, being in majority, pronounced in favor of Abraham Lincoln, of Illinois, the exponent of their sectional views. Under these circumstances, the Southern States threaten to secede from the Union. They allege that the civil compact they made with the Northern States in 1789, guaranteeing equal rights to both, and equal protection to all, has been violated. They further allege that, being in a minority in the Confederacy, they can oppose no legal barrier to the anti-slavery sentiments of the North, which, carried into legislation, will confiscate their property, and even involve their lives.

RÉSUMÉ.

This closes, my Lord, the brief retrospect of our Federal history. I trust it is lucid, as I believe it to be unbiased. It thus appears that, from the first Presidency to the last, the public men of the North and South have differed in their notions of policy.

It also appears that these differences ran so high in the case of the Embargo Act, 1807, that the New England States, whose commercial interests were injured, were on the verge of seceding from the Confederacy.

It likewise appears that the Southern States, to the detriment of their interests, voted for a Tariff and a Bank, 1816, in order to resuscitate the Federal Government and conciliate the Eastern States.

It furthermore appears that the Southern States, finding themselves oppressed by the extreme Tariff policy of the North, threatened, through South Carolina, 1832, to nullify the Federal laws.

It finally appears that the various points of national policy discussed by our public men of the North and South, having been successively disposed of by the popular voice, the politicians of the North, in spite of compromises, thought fit to reopen the abstract question of slavery, in 1854.

• SLAVERY.

I have already said, my Lord, that the interests of England are so intimately blended with this country as to make our welfare a matter of the liveliest solicitude to her statesmen and people. Not only are we by far your best customers, but we are also the producers of that precious staple, upon whose steady culture the commercial supremacy of England depends.

I deem it, therefore, of paramount importance that your Lordship should fully understand the nature and extent of the agitation now shaking this country to its centre. It will be impossible to measure it by any thing that has occurred in England within your Lordship's experience. Fortunately for her, African Slavery never became identified with her social and political existence, as it has with us, and therefore it was an easy task for her public men to look calmly on the subject, and decide upon its fate by a vote of twenty millions sterling. If it were with us, my Lord, as it was with you, a simple financial question, it would be a short solution whether it was worth retaining, or not. But it is far otherwise, as I will undertake to show. To make the Slave question in the United States, with all its complications, more properly appreciated by your Lordship, it will be necessary to go back to its origin, which belongs to our colonial epoch. This, however, is so intimately blended with the history of African Slavery in England, that your Lordship will suffer me, I trust, to venture on a brief sketch of the rise and growth of the Guinea trade. From this it will be seen at a glance, that mere calculations of profit led to the importation of the African into the American Colonies; and I think it may be as clearly perceived that self-interest, even more than humanity, had to do with the abandonment of the traffic.

If, then, it can be established, my Lord, that commercial motives, much more than a tardy philanthropy, effected a revolution of opinion in England on African Slavery; then it may be inferred that the same invincible motives of self-interest will lead, at an early day, to a decided reaction on this subject. As a prelude to this history of African Slavery, it may be interesting to glance, for a moment, at the condition of the White Slave or Serf, in England, scarcely three centuries since.

WHITE SLAVERY IN ENGLAND.

It may be a trite reflection, my Lord, but not an irrelevant one at this moment, to remark that the history of mankind is but a history of slavery, as regards the mass of the people; and the absolute slavish condition of far the greater portion of the population of the world at the present day, manifests clearly enough, if not the tyrannical disposition of man, at least the striking mental inequality of different races and classes, which leads to the subjugation of the vast majority to the superior intelligence of the comparative few. The civilization of Europe, however, has established its supremacy over all others, by the gradual emancipation of the lower class from the most degraded slavery to equality before the law.

It is a singular fact, allow me to add, that of all races of men, the Anglo-Saxon has raised himself from the lowest depths of servitude to the highest forms of civilization; and to him belongs the exclusive distinction and vast renown of being the pioneer of civil liberty. His robust body, industrious character, and vigorous intellect seem to have fitted him especially for the task of his physical and political redemption; and these peculiar traits have lost nothing of their original excellence amid the luxuries of the civilization he has mainly created.

The origin of English serfdom may be fairly dated from the subjugation of ancient Britain by Cæsar, just previous to the Christian era, who found it an easy task, with his well-trained hosts, to reduce a warlike but savage people to an abject state of bondage. Nor was the enterprise more difficult for the free and martial Saxons, just four centuries later, to expel the remains of Roman power, and establish, on a permanent foundation, their own rude forms of government. During the whole period of the Heptarchy, some four centuries more, the degraded inhabitants of Britain remained in the same condition of unmitigated servitude. The slave or villein born on the land of the lords, was attached to it and sold with it. These wore iron collars on their necks, inscribed with the name of the owner. To this category of rural slaves, must be added the large numbers enslaved in civil feuds, as well as those sold by their parents as a means of subsistence. In the seventh century, some Northumbrian slaves were sent to Rome for sale by a speculator, and when exhibited in the slave market, attracted, by their noble appearance and athletic frames, the admiration of Pope Gregory, who sent Augustine, with a suite of missionaries, to convert so striking a people to Christianity.

At the date of the Conquest, 1066, the English Slave Trade was very general and active. Ireland, at that time, was the chief market for export, but the various cities of Europe also kept up a brisk demand. The Doomsday Book, prepared by order of the Conqueror, affords abundant indications of the condition of slavery at this epoch, and of the activity of the domestic Slave Trade. There was a tax imposed at this period by all the cities, as a source of revenue, of four pennies on every slave sold. No female slave was allowed to marry without the consent of the owner. The child of a female slave was also a slave. A freeman who married a slave, reduced himself to her condition; and all slaves were sold and treated like other property. There seems never to have been a law, my Lord, to authorize the holding of slaves. It appears always to have been regarded as a natural right. All the laws that have ever been enacted on the subject, were to emancipate. In A. D. 1102, the Council of Westminster made laws, or canons, against the export of slaves, but with little effect, since the Trade still continued active for a century later. The merchants of Bristol, in order to keep up their supplies, were in the habit of buying children of their parents or of kidnappers. The first serious check the foreign trade received, was in a resolution of the Irish, in 1172, to set free their slaves, and to buy no more at any price. The export of English slaves languished from this period, and finally ceased. The domestic trade, however, continued active. In 1195, the Archbishop of Canterbury gave ten slaves to the Prior of Rochester, as part of the price of the manor of Lambeth, where his Grace's palace stands at the present day.

The right to buy and sell slaves continued centuries later, although the trade itself slowly declined. The class of slaves attached to the soil, called *natives*, were transferable with it, but were occasionally emancipated on various conditions, sometimes as rewards, yet more frequently for sums of money. In 1338, King Edward sold freedom to many slaves, to raise money. In 1381, the insurrection of Wat Tyler, momentarily successful, extorted a charter of freedom from Edward III. for all slaves; but this was almost immediately revoked, and the slaves forced to return to their former condition. The thirst for emancipation began to increase steadily, and constant sales of freedom to bondsmen were taking place. The value of slaves, however, continued high, which is corroborated by an incident that happened in Kent. A certain Simon Burley there demanded no less than 300 lbs. of silver as the price of freedom for one of his slaves. This was thought exorbitant, and the seizure of the man by his master to remove him to another county, was resisted by the populace, and an insurrection ensued. Following the tendency of the epoch, emancipations became more and more frequent. In 1514, Henry VIII., to supply his exchequer, sold freedom to two of his slaves; viz.: to Henry Knight, a tailor, and to John Erle, of the county of Cornwall. This act of manumission begins, "Whereas, originally God created all men free," &c. These are nearly the words used in our own Declaration of Independence, upwards of two centuries later. The process of manumission went rapidly on, and when, in 1574, Queen Elizabeth commissioned Lord Burghley and her Chancellor, Sir Walter Mildmay, to compound with the serfs upon her manors for their freedom, it may be said that the slavery of the lower classes of England had well-nigh reached its extinction. Thus it may be seen,

2

that the Anglo-Saxon race did not remain, like the African, for countless ages in a savage state, free, but without progress. On the contrary, it emerged from the lowest condition of villeinage, and asserted its intellectual and moral vigor by breaking through all the heavy trammels that surrounded it. Nor did its energies expire with the successful struggle for emancipation, and relapse, like the African, into barbaric sloth; but it has gone on, through every phase of development, till its power and knowledge has encircled the globe. I trust your Lordship will regard with leniency this somewhat stale reiteration of familiar facts, but I thought their repetition, at this particular juncture, was appropriate, and would add, by contrast, not a little interest to the significant history of African Slavery in England that I now propose very briefly to venture on.

RÉSUMÉ.

Anciently, all English labor was enslaved.

Emancipation grew as free labor was found more profitable than slave labor.

The mental energy of the people forced emancipation, and this in spite of ages of prior servitude.

The national productions, capital, and power increased with the progress of emancipation.

The emancipation was gradual through centuries, causing no shock to society.

BLACK SLAVERY IN ENGLAND.

The last phase of African Slavery in the British Dominions, must still be familiar to your Lordship; for it was the Cabinet of Earl Grey, of which your Lordship was the Foreign Secretary, that brought in the Act of Emancipation in May, 1833. Its introduction, however, into the British Colonies is so remote, and the details of its history so seldom recalled, that your Lordship can hardly be supposed to bear either in recollection, amid the more weighty matters pressing on your attention. As it is necessary to my purpose, may I be permitted, in as brief a digest as possible, to glance over the striking, and, to our present tastes, really shocking incidents connected with the African Trade?

It is very singular, my Lord, that almost at the same moment the last traces of serfdom were disappearing from England, the enslavement of another and distant race should spring up. Such, however, is the fact; for it was in 1561 that Sir John Hawkins fitted out three small vessels, of from forty to sixty tons each, with which, laden with English merchandise, he sailed for the Guinea Coast, where he exchanged his wares for a cargo of Negroes, that he carried thence to Hispaniola, and sold them for hides, sugar, and ginger, with which he returned to England. This was the humble commencement of the trade in African Blacks that was carried on by England, with immense profits, for the long period of two hundred and forty-six years. The success of Hawkins' adventure seems to have had the same effect on that day, as the gold discoveries on the present. The Continent of Africa was speedily reported to be filled with Blacks, to be had for the mere catching; and that they could be sold at great advantage in the West Indies. Expeditions were fitted out rapidly one after another, and British enterprise and capital were soon actively employed in prosecuting this lucrative traffic. In 1689, the British Government entered into a convention with Spain, by which she agreed to provide her West India dependencies with African slaves. In 1713, the celebrated "South Sea Company," of London, also undertook, by convention, to supply Spain with black slaves; and these were regularly furnished, at the rate of 4,800 per annum, for thirty years. The trade grew apace, and finally took such proportions that Gen. O'Hara, Governor of Senegambia, reported, in 1760, that in the "previous fifty years, no less than 70,000 Blacks had been deported per annum from that country alone." This makes an aggregate of 3,500,000, a very startling number, certainly, for that age. Your Lordship will remember that the British West Indies were the chief destination of these Blacks, and that Jamaica continued the principal depot during the eighteenth century. In the gradual development of this vast commerce, there were three great Interests that especially prospered: First, the Manufacturers who supplied the goods for the African trade; next, the Shipping which conducted it; and last, but not least, the Merchants of London, Bristol, and Liverpool, who carried it on.

The Planters in the Colonies profited greatly by the supply of labor, but, at length, they became alarmed at the extraordinary influx of the Blacks, who began greatly to outnumber the Whites. The danger that was naturally apprehended from this source induced the Colonial authorities, finally, to impose such a tax (£10 per head) as they supposed would check the evil. This immediately drew forth an energetic remonstrance from the Manufacturers, Shippers, and Merchants, to the Imperial Parliament, in 1774, against the duty in question. The Colonial agent in London, however, earnestly represented the necessity of putting some restraint on the trade. The Colony of Virginia, at the same time, also sent up to Parliament similar representations as to their case. The Government, however, considered it the most profitable policy to favor the interests of the Slave Merchants and Shippers, and therefore decided against any interference with them. The colonial duty of £10 was abrogated, and the Trade was consequently prosecuted with renewed vigor.

It was about this period that the political connection between the mother country and her American colonies was broken off, and one of the first uses made of their new independence by the Southern States, was the attempt to put a stop to the African Slave Trade, in order to check the increase of Blacks. After great effort, the Southern States succeeded in obtaining the consent of the New England States to give up the slave traffic in 1808. It was likewise at this period the recently emancipated people of France declared, in the height of their revolutionary fervor, that all classes and races of men were free and equal; and the frightful massacres of St. Domingo were the early result of the application of such ideas to the Blacks.

Your Lordship will please to bear in mind, that while these events were transpiring in America and France, a new doctrine of the equality of the Black and White began to be broached in England. The first apostle of this novel opinion was Mr. Wilberforce, and in 1788, a year after the United States Constitution had prospectively abolished the Slave Trade, he gave notice in Parliament that he intended to bring in a Bill relative to the Slave Trade. On this occasion, the leaders on both sides of the House, Mr. Pitt and Mr. Fox, favored the movement. In the February following, the Privy Council ordered a Committee to inquire into the state of the Trade, and a long and interesting report was made. Among the evidence produced, was a letter to Lord Hawkesbury, from Mr. Gustavus Vassa, Commissary of the African Settlement, that contained a declaration which, beyond all doubt, was the germ of that change of opinion in England against Black Slavery which soon after set in. He stated that, in his opinion, if the Slave Trade were abolished, Africa would soon become a market for British manufactures superior to all Europe. "If the Blacks," to use his own language, "are permitted to remain in their own country, they will double in every fifteen years, and in proportion to such increase will be the demand for British goods." There was more evidence of the same character, and the new school of Wilberforce readily laid hold of such arguments to induce the manufacturers and merchants to give up the Trade. On the other hand, emphatic evidence was adduced, on high authority, that went to show the Africans were nothing but irreclaimable barbarians, incapable of civilization ; with no idea of landed property, and cursed with an incurable indolence. The Government, fearing to disturb an old and profitable commerce, after deliberation, adopted the latter view, and again encouraged the Trade by new regulations. The law passed, as your Lordship may recollect, in 1799 (twelve years after our Constitution had abolished the Trade), was of such a nature that it might be properly qualified as the "Slave Trade

Charter," but, in fact, it was entitled an act "To regulate the carrying of Slaves in British vessels from the west coast of Africa to the West Indies." Among the regulations of this new statute, was one, doubtless in the interests of humanity, to the effect that each slave vessel should have painted conspicuously on her stern the words, "Allowed to carry Slaves." But there was another provision, much more striking, and it ran thus :— "No loss by mortality of Slaves, whether natural, or the consequence of ill-treatment, or *by throwing them overboard*, shall be recoverable by any Policy of Insurance." The "throwing overboard," thus gravely recognized as a *legal right*, had, during a century and a half, been so customary that the Insurance Companies were heavy losers; and to protect them against these frauds, the present clause was enacted, which forbid the owners to recover.

It is scarcely credible that, in your Lordship's lifetime, such a state of things as this could have existed in any civilized country, or that such horrible barbarity could have been regarded by the Government and people of England with utter indifference. But it was likewise at this period, it must be remembered, that the death-penalty was so liberally distributed by the laws of England, that every petty thief was quickly transported from the prison to Tyburn. This sanguinary spirit was, doubtless, a relic of those bloody civil wars that had so often desolated fair England. From these excesses a reaction was natural; and such extraordinary strides have been made in the last fifty years towards a higher humanity, that we find at the present day, in London, a "Society for the Prevention of Cruelty to Animals," and frequent prosecutions are instituted, in its name, against the ill-treatment of cats and dogs. Would that some such institution had existed only fifty years ago, when its energies might have been humanely directed against the owners of slaves for "throwing them overboard" at sea; but they would have intrenched themselves, no doubt, behind the sanction of Parliament, which only forbid them recovering any compensation for doing so. Truly, my Lord, when these two epochs are contrasted, and both within the same century and the same country, the notion is almost forced upon us that cruelty and humanity, brutality and refinement, are little else than fashions of the day, which come in and go out pretty much as interest or fancy may dictate.

This was the condition of the British Slave Trade when this century opened. But the Planters in the Colonies resolutely continued their opposition to it; and the Abolitionists, led by Mr. Wilberforce, were actively representing to the Manufacturing and Mercantile interests the large market that would certainly spring up in Africa on the cessation of the Trade, which the United States and France had already abolished. The combination of Planters and Abolitionists, reinforced tardily by the Manufacturers, were at length sufficient, with the example set by other countries, to induce the British Government, not long before your Lordship, if I remember, entered office, to abolish the Slave Trade in 1807. Thus, after two hundred and forty-six years of uninterrupted activity, the Trade was brought to an end.

With your Lordship's leave, I will copy from Parliamentary Reports some brief account of the Trade in its days of prosperity. During the eighteenth century there were imported, according to official returns, 1,128,400 Blacks into Jamaica; and at the close of the century there were but 350,000 Blacks on the Island. The value put on the Negroes, by the reports, was £30, or $150, per head. Under the industry of these Blacks, the Exports of the Island, towards the close of the century, amounted to £5,400,000, or 27 millions of dollars per annum. The Island itself was valued at twelve years' purchase, say £64,800,000. The working capacity of a Negro during his service was estimated at 8 times his cost; or, in other words, the average product of a hand during his life was £240, or $1200. The number of Blacks carried to all the British West Indies, up to the close of the eighteenth century, was calculated at 2,728,400. The cost of these, at the average, would be £81,852,000, and their aggregate production £654,816,000, or $3,274,080,000! Of this vast sum, little or nothing remained on the Island where it was produced. The

Blacks, that were obtained on the Coast in exchange for Lancashire goods, were "worked up" into sugar, coffee, rum, &c.,
which were sent to the owners in London and Bristol.

After the Abolition of the Trade, the West India Planters
discovered that to keep up production required a regular
foreign supply of labor, for the natural increase of the Blacks
did not answer their anticipations. Not long after this, the
followers of Mr. Wilberforce began to agitate a new theory—
the emancipation of the Blacks in the West Indies. They
endeavored to enlist in their support the Manufacturing and
Shipping interests, by representing, first, that free Blacks
would produce more than Slaves; and next, they would consume a larger amount of British goods. Such results would,
therefore, give more employment to British vessels, it was
argued, than the Slave Trade had ever done. In this way the
Wilberforce Party gradually won over to their untried theories
the Manufacturing and Commercial interests.

They next turned their attention to winning proselytes in
other classes of the community. Constant and skilful appeals
were made to the religious and moral sentiments of the English
people, and immense numbers of tracts were circulated. Works
of fiction were frequently composed to inflame the public
mind, and at length the Pulpit took up the theme. Numerous
Societies were formed to hasten on the Emancipation of the
Blacks in the West Indies; but soon this new-born philanthropy
took a wider field. Branches of these Societies were established in other countries, more especially in the United States.
The Sunday-schools of New England were selected as the first
lever for effecting the Emancipation of the Blacks in the
Southern States. The leading minds of England began seriously to entertain the theory, and I believe your Lordship
and other prominent Statesmen were converts to it, that the
free Black would work as well as the free White, and that
what had been true of Serf labor in England might be equally
true of Black labor everywhere. Hence it was inferred that
the West Indies might become a thriving collection of free
Black Colonies, and that the market for British goods (John

Bull never forgets profit in philanthropy) would soon exceed all anticipation. It was thought that if the United States could be brought to entertain the same conviction, our Southern States would ere long be converted into a great free Black cotton-growing country, whose alliance with England would be all the closer from identity of interest and policy. But if it should turn out otherwise, it was argued by the zealots of that day, and the Northern States should adopt the new British view of Emancipation, while the Southern States refused to try the experiment, why, the worst that could happen would be the dissolution of the Confederacy, which would relieve England and Europe from any further dread of the Great Republic.

Opinions so plausible as these soon took deep root in the public mind, and the cause of manumission made rapid strides. On May 15, 1823, Sir Fowel Buxton, the colleague of Wilberforce, gave notice of a Bill to extinguish Slavery in the West Indies, and Parliament, at once, decided that measures should be taken to ameliorate the moral condition of the Blacks, so as to prepare them for freedom.

In a Circular of July 9, 1823, Lord Bathurst communicated these resolutions of Parliament to the Colonists, and enjoined them to conform thereto. The intentions of the Government filled the Planters with alarm, and awoke the liveliest resistance. They declared their interests would not only be sacrificed, but that the Colonies would be ruined, for they pronounced the theory of free Black labor a miserable delusion.

These remonstrances were unheeded. As soon as the Blacks became aware of the designs of the Government, insurrections began to break out, and there was danger of the horrors of St. Domingo being renewed by a general massacre of the Whites. The Government, therefore, determined to press on its scheme of Emancipation. It began, in 1831, by decreeing the freedom of the Slaves on all the Crown lands, against the most energetic opposition of the Planters. Finally, in May, 1833, Lord Stanley brought in the Bill for the abolition of Slavery. It was adopted by the Commons, June 12, 1833, and by the Lords on the 25th of the same month, receiving the sanction of the Crown, August 28, 1833.

The Bill provided, that all slaves six years old at the date of August 1, 1834, should pass into the condition of Apprentices of three classes : 1st, Rural laborers attached to the soil ; 2d, Rural laborers unattached ; 3d, Laborers not rural. The first two classes were to serve as Apprentices for six years, and the last for four years.

The number of slaves was found to be 780,933, and their value was taken to be the average of the sales from 1822 to 1830, or £56 per head. The average working time of a Black was estimated at 8 years ; and it was calculated, by giving the Planter 4 and 6 years of his time, the Black paid four-sevenths of his value in labor. The remaining three-sevenths, or £25 per head, it was proposed to pay in money, and for this purpose £20,000,000, or one hundred millions of dollars, was voted by Parliament. This well-intended combination, meant to please everybody, ended by pleasing none. The Black murmured, and demanded instant freedom ; and his forced, discontented labor was so unprofitable, that the Planters finally abandoned the remainder of the term.

Full soon the great fact became apparent, that the free Black would not work at all. The boasted theory that flourishing free Black Colonies would build up a vast market for British goods was proved every year to be more and more fallacious. As there was no industry in production, it followed there was no market for consumption. The natural, inherent indolence of the Black could not be overcome for those rewards of industry which stimulate the White, but which experience shows the Black does not appreciate. When the demonstration became irresistible that the free Black could not be induced to work, the British Government had to choose between the utter ruin of the West India Colonies, or the creation of some new kind of labor. Hence the origin of the present Coolie Trade. The solicitations of the Planters became so pressing, that an Order in Council was issued, Jan. 15, 1842 (only nine years after Black Emancipation), which allowed the emigration of

East Indian *Coolies* (day-laborers), under certain Government restrictions. The Chinese Coolie Trade is in the hands of Ship-owners, who employ Chinese contractors to collect these miserable creatures, and ship them to Peru and Cuba under circumstances of great barbarity. English vessels are chiefly engaged in this traffic, the horrors of which fully equal, if they do not exceed, those of the former Slave Trade.

I will not weary your Lordship with further details on this subject. It is plain, however, that the Emancipationists of England have little, unhappily, to congratulate themselves upon in the way of humanity, by substituting the present Coolie Trade for the late Black Slave Trade. One instance of many will suffice. The British bark Gertrude arrived at Havana, May 13, 1853. She had started on her voyage with a cargo of 192 Coolies, and of these 152 had died during the passage. I do not know if the Coolies are insured now-a-days as the Blacks used to be, else this extraordinary mortality might be suspected. The survivors, however, were sold for 7 years to the Planters, and were turned, of course, into the Negro gangs, to be governed by the same discipline. At the end of the term of 7 years, it should be added, the Coolie is turned adrift to perish, or, if still able to work, he is employed, like the Negroes, for a bare subsistence. The Coolie Trade is not merely a revival of the old Slave Trade, but something worse. The new treaty with China makes the Coolie Trade, for the first time, legal.

The facts I have related, my Lord, have carried the conviction home to the minds of the practical men of England, that *free Black labor is a mere illusion!* Consequently, we find the London Times, and other organs of public opinion, are beginning to admit, unreservedly, that Emancipation in the West Indies was a failure and a mistake: that humanity has gained nothing, while all other interests have lost.

The Manufacturers of Lancashire, too, are unable to conceal their apprehensions at the spread of the exploded English theory of free Black labor now entertained so generally in our Northern States. They feel their dependence increasing every year on our cotton crop of the South, and they naturally dread lest the tampering of the North with Black labor in the South may lead, sooner or later, to irregular or diminished supplies of this indispensable element of British Manufactures.

I will now proceed, my Lord, to consider Black Slavery in the United States.

RÉSUMÉ.

During 246 years, England derived vast commercial profits from the African Slave Trade.

The Trade directly interested the shipping-merchants of Liverpool, London, and Bristol, and the manufacturers of "coast goods," while the national wealth greatly increased under the influx of West India productions.

The Trade was stopped only when larger benefits were expected from free African colonies than from dealing in Slaves.

Emancipation was, finally, determined on when free Black colonies were supposed more advantageous than Slave colonies.

The theory of free Black colonies utterly failed, through the inherent and incurable indolence of the Blacks.

The Abolition of the Slave Trade, and the Emancipation of the Blacks in the West Indies, may have been inspired by philanthropy, but the moral question was necessarily subsidiary to calculations of interest.

The failure of West India Emancipation is rapidly effecting a change of opinion in the leading minds of England as to the feasibility of free Black labor in the cotton-growing States of America.

BLACK SLAVERY IN THE UNITED STATES.

From what I have already stated, it may be seen, my Lord, that during the colonial existence of this country, African Slavery had been introduced and overspread its whole surface. The Southern Colonies had, from the fertility of the soil and the value of their productions, become the most profitable mart for Black labor, but the influx gradually outstripped their productive powers, and began, as elsewhere, to inspire the leading men of this section with serious alarm. They devised what means they could to check it, but commercial rapacity eluded or overpowered their remonstrances. While the Southern Colonies were thus suffering, at this early date, both inconvenience and detriment from the Blacks who were forced upon them, the Northern, or New England Colonies, were driving a brisk and profitable business upon the solitary basis of the African Slave Trade. The principal occupations of these Colonies consisted of Commerce and the Fisheries. The New England ships made the voyage to England with tobacco, rice, and other Southern products, and then took in British manufactures for the Gold Coast, which exchanging for Blacks, they returned with them to the Southern Colonies, sold them, and reloaded with tobacco, &c., for the North and Europe, as before, thus completing the round voyage. The fisheries employed a considerable number of persons, and the cured fish found sale chiefly in the Catholic countries of Europe, mostly in exchange for coin,* which was always in demand for England. Large quantities of these fish were sold in the West Indies for sugar and molasses. The latter was distilled into rum, which, in the changing character of the Slave Trade on the Coast under the British governors, rapidly became a favorite article of barter for Blacks, greatly to the dissatisfaction of the English manufacturers of coast-goods. Lord Sheffield, in his report to the Parliamentary Committee of 1777, states, that " out of the Slavers which periodically left Boston, thirteen of them were loaded with rum only, and that having exchanged this for 2,888 Negroes with the governors of the Gold Coast, they carried them thence to the Southern Colonies." The same report mentions that during the three years ending with 1770, New England had sent 270,147 gallons of rum to the Gold Coast. Thus, from what I have stated, the startling fact will be elicited, my Lord, that the Northern and Southern

---

* These were almost the only coins that circulated in those Colonies at that time, and consisted of Joes, Half-Joes, Pistoles, &c.

Colonies, long before the breaking out of the Revolutionary War, were engaged in a lively controversy on the subject of slavery; the South resisting the excessive flow of Blacks into their section, and New England persisting in the importation for the profits of the trade. The South was anxious to stop the Slave Trade and manumit their Blacks, but New England, like the Mother Country, was not disposed to listen to them, and abandon so lucrative a traffic.

Mr. Jefferson, of Virginia, seems to have been one of the most earnest advocates of the Southern sentiment. In 1777, being then a member of the Virginia Legislature, he brought in a bill which became a law, "to prevent the importation of slaves." He also proposed a system of general emancipation, as a preliminary to which he introduced a bill to authorize manumission, and this became a Law. In these efforts he had the support and sympathy of the Slaveholding States who were overrun with slaves, that returned no adequate remuneration. At this period their numbers reached some 600,000, a part of whom were employed in raising tobacco and rice. The majority of them, however, were occupied in domestic farm-labor, producing no exportable values. Hence there was no profit in slavery at the South, while at the North it was even a greater burden. Massachusetts found it so unproductive that, in 1780, she abolished it in her own borders, but she did not cease for that reason to force it, by her importations, on the South.

In the Congress of the Confederation, the views of the North and South on the subject of slavery, founded on interests so antagonistic, frequently came into collision. It was at this epoch, too, that Virginia, Georgia, and other Southern States, ceded to the Federal Government, for the common benefit of all the States, their immense Western territories.* All the States were then Slaveholding, and the idea that a man could not hold his slaves in any part of the territory of the United States, had never yet been broached. On the contrary, the right to carry them everywhere was undoubted. The policy of

---

* The State of Virginia, March, 1784, ceded the territory north of the Ohio, on the

Virginia, however, was manumission; and Mr. Jefferson, in 1784, prepared in the Congress of the Confederation a clause preventing slaves being carried into the said territories ceded to the United States, north of the Ohio river. This was a part of the Southern scheme of manumission, which was meant as a check to the trading in Negro-slaves, carried on by Massachusetts with unabated activity. This clause did not pass at the time, but, in 1787, it was renewed by Nathan Dane in the Federal Convention. The clause enjoining the restitution of fugitive slaves was then added, and it passed unanimously. By an unanimous vote it became a vital part of the Federal Constitution, and without it this compact could never have gone into effect. The Slave Trade carried on by the North became, also, the theme of much sharp discussion in the Convention. The North was not disposed, of course, to give it up, but with the South it had become an intolerable grievance. They had long and earnestly protested against it when carried on by the Mother Country, but their minds were now made up to break with the North rather than submit further to this traffic. The North then demanded compensation for the loss of this very thriving trade, and the South readily conceded it by granting them the monopoly of the coasting and carrying trade against all foreign tonnage. In this way it was settled that the Slave Trade should be abolished after 1808.* Without this important

condition that it be divided into not more than five, and not less than *three* States. Out of this territory was formed—

Ohio,	Nov.,	1802		
Indiana,	April,	1816		
Illinois,	Dec.,	1818	North of the Ohio	land ceded by Virginia.
Michigan,	Feb.,	1833		
Wisconsin,	Jan.,	1838		
Kentucky,	June,	1791	South of the Ohio	

The Tennessee land was ceded by N. Carolina.

Mississippi   "   "   S. Carolina.

Alabama   "   "   S. Carolina and Georgia.

* In corroboration of the above, I append the following extract from the sermon of Rev. Dr. N. Adams, of the Essex-street church, Boston, delivered on Fast Day, January 4, 1861:

"We at the North are certainly responsible before God for the existence of slavery in our land. The Committee of the Convention which framed the Constitution of the United States consisted of Messrs. Rutledge of South Carolina, Randolph of Vir-

clause, the South would never have consented to enter into a Confederacy with the North. The Federal Constitution, with these essential clauses, having passed into operation, it became, henceforth, a certainty that the Slave Trade would finally expire in the United States at the close of 1808. This left it still a duration of nineteen years, and the North seemed determined to reap the utmost possible advantage from the time remaining. The Duke de Rochefoucault-Liancourt, in his work on the United States, 1795, states, that "Twenty vessels from the harbors of the North are engaged in the importation of slaves into Georgia; they ship one Negro for every ton burden." Thus we see, my Lord, that while New England was vigorously engaged in buying and selling Negro-slaves, Virginia, on the other hand, was steadfastly pursuing her theory of manumission.

In 1793, Congress, on the recommendation of President Washington, passed an act to put in force the clause of the Constitution enjoining the restoration of fugitive slaves. It seems evident they were regarded by the Constitution in the light of Property only. It likewise provided for taxing them, and ordained that three-fifths of their number should be a basis of representation. This was, certainly, the view taken by the framers of the Constitution, in their intercourse with foreign nations. John Adams, afterwards President, and Doctor Franklin signed, in 1783, the Treaty of Peace with Great Britain, which contained provision for payment of "Slaves and other Property" carried away during the War. These Treaties were examined and approved by the Government, composed

---

ginia, and three from Free States, viz., Messrs. Wilson of Pennsylvania, Gorham of Massachusetts, and Ellsworth of Connecticut. They reported as a section for the Constitution, that no tax or other duty should be laid on the migration or importation of such persons as the several States should think proper to admit; not that such migration or importation should be prohibited. This was referred by the Convention to a committee, a majority of whom being from the Slave States, they reported that the Slave Trade be abolished after 1800, and that a tax be levied on imported slaves. But in the Convention, the Free States of Massachusetts, New Hampshire, and Connecticut, voted to extend the trade eight years, and it was accordingly done; by means of which it is estimated there are now at least three hundred thousand more slaves in the country than there would otherwise have been."

also of the very men who had taken the leading part in drafting the Constitution. In the Treaty of Peace at Ghent, in 1815, the same clause recurred, and the British Government paid a million and a half of dollars for Slaves that had been carried off by the enemy. The accounts of Hon. Richard Rush, when Secretary of the Treasury, contain the various sums paid by the United States Government to the "Owners of Slaves and other Property." Our Government has also made frequent demands for the payment of Slave-property since the Peace. I remember that while I was an *attaché* to our Legation in London, some twenty years since, the American Minister, Mr. Andrew Stevenson, conducted a negotiation with your Lordship, then Foreign Secretary, for the payment of sundry slaves that had been cast ashore from wrecked American vessels, and set free by the Authorities of Bermuda. The demand was finally acknowledged, and the sum of £23,500 was paid as an indemnity. In a word, the action of the Federal Government has been uniform and consistent in asserting and protecting the rights of our Slave-owners against all Foreign Powers. The right to this Property has been just as positively recognized in our domestic relations. In all the State Conventions held to discuss the Federal Constitution prior to adopting it, the right of property in slaves was never contested. The law at that time for recovering that property, was of a summary nature. The owner might seize his property wherever he found it, and on making an affidavit before a Federal Judge, a warrant was issued for the removal of it. There was no provision for trial by jury, or for writ of *Habeas Corpus*, which would be indispensable if Black Slaves were considered as Persons.

In 1797, John Adams, who signed the Treaty of Peace, and was the leader of the New England or Federal Party, succeeded Washington in the Presidential chair. At this period, the Slavery question was frequently agitated by the Democratic party of the South, with a view to its modification. In 1800, Jan. 2, Mr. Waln, of Philadelphia, presented a petition to Congress, from the free Blacks of Philadelphia, praying for a

3

revision of the Fugitive Slave Law. On this occasion, Mr. Harrison Gray Otis, a leader of the Federal party, thus expressed himself: "Although he possessed no slaves himself," he said, "yet he saw no reason why others might not; and that their owners, and not Congress, were the fittest persons to regulate that *species of property*." Mr. Brown, of Rhode Island, on the same occasion, declared "that the petition was not from Negroes, but was the contrivance of a combination of *Jacobins* (meaning the Democratic party), who had troubled Congress for many years, and he feared would never cease to do so. He therefore moved that the petition be taken away by those who had brought it there." The motion being supported by Messrs. Gallatin, Dana, and other Northern members, the petition was withdrawn. In this debate, the Northern members who represented the Slave-trading interests, naturally adhered to the Property in Blacks, although the new doctrine of the British Abolitionists began to make converts in this country, outside of the body of Quakers, who had always opposed slavery.

It may be as well to remark here, my Lord, that it does not appear any laws were ever enacted in Great Britain, authorizing the trading in, or possession of Black Slaves as Property. Nevertheless, that they were so regarded, is evident from the opinion of the Eleven Crown Judges, given in pursuance of an Order in Council, and in consequence of which the Navigation Act was extended to the Slave Trade, to the exclusion of Aliens. The laws by which England allowed the holding of slaves, extended, of course, to the Colonies; and all those of North America held slaves, without any special enactments for that purpose. The right was inherent, like that to any property; and when the separation of the Colonies from the Mother Country took place, that legal right, like the Common Law of England, survived the Revolution, and remained in force in all parts of the country. It may seem, to your Lordship, unnecessary to dwell so emphatically on this point; but it is the very pivot of the dispute now raging in the United States. It is claimed by the Anti-slavery party that slavery exists by local law only, and cannot exist out of the State sanctioning it.

Whereas, it is maintained by their opponents that it originally existed all over the land, whether as Colonies, or States, and that it required a special law to exclude it. This fact is beyond cavil.* It should be also recollected that the Spanish and French Colonies, that afterwards became a part of the United States, derived the right to hold slaves from the head of the Church, as well as from the State.

To return to the record of events. During Mr. Jefferson's first term of office, the State of Virginia proposed to the Federal Government that the proceeds of the public lands that had been ceded to it should be appropriated to the manumission and removal of slaves, with the sanction of the respective States. This movement was not successful.

It is necessary to notice two very important events that occurred during the Administration of Mr. Jefferson, which wholly changed the destiny of Black Slavery in the United States. The first was the invention of the Cotton-gin,† which gave great additional value to this staple, and hence opened a broader field to the employment of the Blacks. The next was the purchase of Louisiana, which added new and valuable territory to the South and its special products. These two events revolutionized completely the value of Slave labor at the South, and the Blacks, instead of continuing a burden as hitherto, became henceforward a source of profit. It followed, of course, that the Slaveholders, instead of seeking, as formerly, to get rid of this kind of property, began to show an anxious desire for its preservation. On the other hand, the approaching termination of the Slave Trade, which had profitably employed for so many years the commercial interests of New England, rendered that section not only indifferent to the

---

* Among other Authorities on this vexed question of the day, may be cited that of Chief-justice Parker, of Massachusetts, the leading Abolition State. In 2 Pickering, he says: "We thus, in making the Constitution, entered into an agreement that slaves should be considered as property," &c., &c., &c.

† This admirable machine for separating the seed from the cotton with extreme celerity, was the invention of Eli Whitney, of Massachusetts. It is strange that it was the mechanical genius of a New Englander that alone prevented the abolition of slavery long since by the South.

prolongation of slavery, but even, out of chagrin from having been forced by the opposition of the South to give it up, they began to nourish a species of spite against it, and which has since manifested itself with uninterrupted bitterness, till, at last, it is bringing the Confederacy to the verge of a final dissolution. Thus we see, my Lord, not only a singular and sudden revulsion of opinion on the subject of slavery in the South and North at the epoch in question, but that in both cases it was dictated by a vital change in their material interests. It appears, then, that mere humanity had nothing to do with the South trying to get rid of slavery, or with the North beginning to oppose it. They were both governed by the same motive of self-interest that had for so long a time stimulated England, first to carry on the Slave Trade, and next to emancipate her Blacks.

The cotton culture now began to develop its influence on the Blacks. Instead of complaints of a vast surplus of hands, there was very soon talk of a scarcity; and year by year the number of bales of cotton raised per head of the Blacks, has increased, until the proportion has reached one and a quarter bales each hand, against one bale for every twenty-four Blacks, sixty years ago. The price of the Blacks has accordingly risen from $250 to $1,500 for good field-hands. The increase has been confined to natural laws since the Abolition of the Trade, in 1808.

The cessation of the Slave Trade, and the purchase of Louisiana, both of which were so distasteful to the North, were followed, unfortunately, as already stated, by the Embargo Act, in Mr. Jefferson's Administration; and all this together, gave nearly a quietus to the commercial interests of New England. The exasperation which followed these measures, that seemed to threaten ruin to this section, led shortly to a desire to break up the Confederacy. In February, 1809, the Governor-general of Canada, Craig, deputed his agent, John Henry, to go to Boston and treat with the leading Federalists there; and by the arrangement then made, Massachusetts was to declare itself independent, and invite a Congress to erect a separate Government. Mr. John Q. Adams, Ex-President, in a letter to Mr. Otis, 1828, states that the plan had been so far matured, that proposals had been made to a certain individual to put himself at the head of the military organization. These schemes went on until they resulted in the Hartford Convention, 1814, where the subject of a Northern Confederacy, in all its bearings, underwent discussion. The sentiment of the North at that time may be seen in the party cry: " The Potomac for a boundary—The Negro States to themselves." This was the favorite phrase of the day all over the Eastern States, and the Secession movement now going on in the South, was not more popular or more seriously resolved on. The Peace with Great Britain soon afterwards occurred, and the stimulus this gave to business of all kinds, together with the conciliatory conduct, as stated, of Mr. Calhoun of South Carolina, diverted New England from her resolute menace to break up the Union.

While this irritation was still lingering in the Northern mind, a bill was introduced into Congress, 1818, to authorize the people of Missouri to form a Constitution, preparatory to admission into the Union. This territory was a portion of that same Louisiana whose purchase had been so vehemently resisted by New England. During its ownership by Spain, and afterwards by France, slavery had existed in the whole of this territory, and it remained undisturbed after its purchase by the United States; nevertheless its admission into the Union as a Slave State, was violently opposed by the Eastern States. An ardent political struggle ensued, that threatened the safety of the Confederacy, but which was, finally, allayed by admitting Missouri as a Slave State, but on the condition that no more Slave States should exist north of the 36° 30' parallel of latitude. This is the well-known Missouri Compromise. It was at this time, also, that the Slave Trade was declared to be Piracy, and punishable with death.

Meanwhile, slavery had become so manifestly unprofitable at the North, that most of these States abolished it. New York did so in 1826, and many other States, even Delaware,

Maryland, and Virginia, were moving in the same direction. New Jersey, Ohio, and Delaware passed resolutions desiring Congress to appropriate the proceeds of the Public Lands to the manumission of slaves, with the consent of the Slave States. In 1825, Rufus King, of New York, made the same proposition in Congress, where it had been originally introduced by Virginia. At this period, in the Southern States the utmost favor was extended to Emancipation. Societies for this purpose were formed to co-operate with the Colonization Society, then in full vigor, and whose object was to free Blacks and transport them to Liberia. In March, 1825, Virginia passed an act to furnish the Colonists in Liberia, under the direction of the "Richmond and Manchester (England) Colonization Society," with implements of husbandry, clothing, &c. The emancipation of Blacks to be sent to Liberia, were frequent all over the Southern States, and on a liberal scale. Alabama, Louisiana, and Missouri passed laws prohibiting slaves to be brought within their borders for sale, and further enacting that those brought in by settlers should not be sold under two years.

The sentiment of Emancipation was making steady progress; but unfortunately, at the same time, a decided repugnance to free Blacks began to manifest itself. Ohio, Illinois, and other Northwestern States forbade by law free Blacks coming into the State, under any pretence; and a white person who brought one in, was required to give bonds in $500. They were not regarded as citizens of the United States, and from their idle habits, were considered as a nuisance everywhere. The Southern States also enacted that free Blacks arriving there as seamen, should be under surveillance while in port. In consequence of this general antipathy to free Blacks, and in view of the difficulty of deporting them, Mr. Tucker, of Virginia, proposed in Congress, 1825, to set off the territory west of the Rocky Mountains as a Colony for free Blacks. This judicious effort failed; but all the leading statesmen of the South, Mr. Mangum, Mr. McDuffie, &c., urged the adoption of some scheme of emancipation.

Up to this period, the Emancipation and Colonization scheme had been gradual, progressive, and beneficial. It had been conducted on wise as well as Christian principles, and certainly with the best results. The organ of this practical enterprise was published at Baltimore, under the title of the " Genius of Universal Gradual Emancipation."

About this time, unhappily, a new movement was initiated in New England. The doctrine of Abolition was then at the zenith of its popularity in England, where it was already proposed to transplant it to our Southern States, which would then be converted into a great free Black cotton-growing country. This utterly impracticable idea was seized upon by various individuals of the New England States, who forthwith began to sow the seeds of agitation. It is impossible to attribute to them any very philanthropic motive ; for only twenty years had elapsed since Massachusetts had been forced to give up her slave-trading, and it is not at all credible that the tastes thus acquired should, in so short a time, have been supplanted by so ardent a love for the Negro of the South as to desire his manumission at the risk of breaking up the Confederacy. No, my Lord, it really looks more like the renewed expression of that old grudge which the Eastern States have for so many years nourished against the South.

Be that as it may, it was in 1828 that a Mr. Arthur Tappan subscribed, with the aid of friends in Boston, sufficient funds to establish a newspaper in New York, called the " Journal of Commerce," whose object was to promote the borrowed English theory of Abolition.* Its Editor was a certain David Hale, an auctioneer of Boston, and a teacher in the Presbyterian Sunday-school there. At the same juncture, the Baltimore " Genius of Emancipation" fell into the hands of another Abolitionist, named W. Lloyd Garrison. This individual was the grandson of what was known as a "Tory" during our Revolutionary War, and who, at the Peace, was compelled to fly the country to Nova Scotia,

* This Journal has long since abandoned its original tenets, and is now a conspicuous stickler for the rights of the South.

whence his widowed daughter and her only son returned, some years after, to Boston, to seek a livelihood. The young Garrison readily caught up the doctrine of Abolition, as most congenial to his English antecedents and education, and set to work with baleful energy to urge its propagation, fraught with so many dangers to the country of his adoption. On assuming the editorship of the Baltimore paper, he instantly assailed both Colonization and Emancipation as only obstructions to Abolition, and openly avowed that the Union of the States was equally an obstacle to Abolition. By some it was supposed that this treasonable denunciation of the Union was out of deference to the memory of his Tory grandfather, who had done all he could to prevent it.

It may easily be imagined that the startling proclamation of such ultra views as these, led rapidly to a complete revolution of feeling at the South. The excitement against Garrison spread far and wide. The Manumission Society of North Carolina demanded his imprisonment, and the State of Georgia set a price upon his head. The emancipation societies at the South began to suspend their operations and to break up. The Baltimore journal mentioned, it was necessary to suppress. The people of the South generally, becoming more and more alarmed at the aggressive attitude of the Abolitionists, began to ponder over some means of defence.

In the year 1830, the same Garrison founded a new journal in Boston, called "The Liberator," whence he propounded his extreme views in the most extravagant language. In the following year, the "New England Anti-slavery Society" was formed. This was followed in due course by the "American Anti-slavery Society," under the leadership of Messrs. Garrison, Tappan, and Birney. The Sunday-schools of the Eastern States became active coadjutors in the same cause. These societies adopted precisely the same tactics as their British prototypes. They circulated tracts and books, full of inflammatory appeals. Highly-colored engravings too, representing the Black undergoing every kind of torture, were distributed for those who could not read. These were meant more especially to excite the Blacks at the South, and were sent through the mails. These proceedings were considered, at the time, so dangerous to the peace of the community and to the integrity of the Union, that popular indignation frequently broke out into riot. In New York, in 1832, the dwelling of Arthur Tappan and the church of Dr. Cox were both demolished by a mob. Many influential citizens sanctioned these violent demonstrations of public feeling, and the well-known Editor of the "Courier and Enquirer," Mr. James Watson Webb, boasted of his share in this rude vindication of Southern rights.*

The Abolitionists of Boston, meanwhile, continued their operations with all the ardor of their puritanical descent. Garrison was sent to England, to obtain funds, by the Anti-slavery Societies; and in 1834 he returned home with Mr. George Thompson, a member of Parliament at that time, and an Abolition lecturer. This led to so violent an outcry, that Thompson, alarmed for his safety, went back to England. A new mode of excitement was then devised by the Abolitionists, who got up a clamor against South Carolina for detaining free Blacks who came into her ports. Massachusetts claimed that free Blacks were her citizens, and that as such they had a right to go to South Carolina; but as she made no complaint against Ohio, Illinois, and other States who also excluded free Blacks, it was evident that she sought a quarrel with South Carolina, for the very purpose of spreading the Abolition infection.

A Mr. Hoar was sent by Massachusetts as an agent to Charleston to make a formal complaint of her alleged grievance, and, as was anticipated, Mr. Hoar was summarily dismissed. Upon this the Abolitionists professed great indignation, and the Legislature was appealed to for a measure of retaliation, which was soon got up under the title of a "Personal Liberty Bill," which was designed, under a transparent plea, to obstruct the restoration of fugitive Blacks.

* This gentleman has since changed his ground, and is now a prominent leader of the Anti-slavery party.

I should not forget here to remark, my Lord, that up to this time, Abolition had been discussed merely as a moral question, but the agitation had gained such strength among its unsuspecting converts, that it was thought high time by its designing leaders to carry it into the political arena, where they anticipated making it a stepping-stone to power and emolument.

It will be seen in the sequel, that these ingenious schemers were doomed to disappointment, and that the *spolia optima* of the agitation they began, were destined to be gathered by the hand of the professional politician, leaving but "a barren sceptre in their gripe."

In 1838, the Abolition party was too weak and too ignorant of political strategy to dare to take the field in person, therefore, they began coquetting with the prominent politicians of the day. Mr. Marcy and Mr. Seward were, at that time, the candidates of the two rival parties for Governor of the State of New York, and perhaps the two most influential men of the North. The occasion was thought opportune by Messrs. Smith and Jay, the New York sponsors for the untoward bantling of Abolition, to put these gentlemen to the test. It happened that there existed a statute in New York, called the "Sojournment Law," which allowed a Slaveholder to bring his Black servants with him, and remain there nine months, without prejudice to his rights; for it had been decided in the Federal Courts that a slave taken *voluntarily* into a Free State, could not be recovered. When Mr. Seward was interrogated in relation to this law, he sustained it as "a becoming act of hospitality to Southern visitors." Mr. Marcy made no reply. Mr. Seward, however, changed his views afterwards on this subject, and refused, in 1840, while Governor, to restore a fugitive slave, on the requisition of Virginia.

The evil results of this sectional issue were foreseen by many States; and among others Ohio, in 1840, passed resolutions in her Legislature to the effect that "Slavery was an institution recognized by the Constitution," and that "the unlawful, unwise, and unconstitutional interference of the fanatical Abolitionists of the North with the institutions of the South, were highly criminal." It may be supposed that the violent proceedings of the Northern Abolitionists did not escape the attention of the South, where they created not only alarm, but aroused a deep and natural feeling of indignation. The change of sentiment that had occurred, may be seen in an act of the State of Alabama, to the effect that "all free Blacks remaining in the State after August 1, 1840, should be enslaved."

At the very close of 1839, a handful of Abolitionists met in Warsaw, N. Y., and decided formally to transform their doctrine from a moral into a political question; and they set to work at once, on a political organization. Determined to eschew any affiliation with the parties of the day, they selected one of their own band, Mr. Birney, as a candidate for the Presidency of the United States. It was now evident to all dispassionate observers, that the motives of the founders of Abolition were not so much the emancipation of the Blacks, as their own elevation to place and power. It is clear enough the North regarded them with just suspicion at that day, for in the Federal election of 1840, Birney received but 7,000 votes.

The agitation of the Slavery question received a new stimulus at this period, from the discussions awakened by the revolt of Texas. This fine country had once formed part of Louisiana, but was ceded by France to Spain, and then became a part of Mexico. In 1836, an insurrection, headed by Americans, broke out, and was soon followed by the independence of Texas. Speculations now ran high in the price of her lands, and the project was broached of reannexing her to the United States. The celebrated Daniel Webster, among others, favored this scheme; but he was afterwards induced to change his views and oppose it. Just as in the case of Louisiana, in 1805, the New England States resisted the Annexation of Texas, during the Presidency of Mr. Tyler, on the same pretext of extending slavery, but on the real ground of jealousy of the South. The leading politicians of the day were sorely embarrassed whether to support Annexation or not; and by opposing it, Mr. Clay lost his election in 1844, and for the same reason, Mr. Van Buren failed to obtain his renomination by the Democratic

party. The difficulty was terminated by the admission of
Texas, March 3, 1845, but on the agreement that four States
should be formed out of the territory, besides the one existing,
and that the States so formed south of the line 36° 30′ should
be admitted with or without Slavery, as their inhabitants
should decide, but that Slavery should not exist north of that
line.

A temporary lull followed; but the Slavery question was
soon again evoked, to gratify a political grudge. The rejection
of Mr. Van Buren as the Democratic candidate in 1844, by
Southern influence, in consequence of his opposition to Texas,
led him, from motives of irritation, to raise up a new party in
New York, on the cry of " Free Soil, or no more Slave States."
This act was a violation of the agreement made with the South
on the admission of Texas, and was frowned upon by the
Democratic party; but the issue started by Mr. Van Buren
was successful enough to divide the party in the State of New
York, and to give the election to the Northern party. As a
matter of course, this incensed and alarmed the South, who
were, at last, pacified by the Compromise measures of 1850,
which, however, were stoutly opposed by Mr. W. H. Seward,
who had become already the chosen and able representative of
the Anti-slavery sentiments of the North.

I may as well observe here, my Lord, what I have already
stated elsewhere, that the politicians of the North, unfortunately, found themselves in the sad predicament of having
no political principles to advocate. The settlement of the
Tariff question in '46, on the demand of the commercial interests of the North, left them wholly destitute of any policy by
which they might hope to ride into power. Under these circumstances, it was natural they should follow with a wistful
eye the labors of the Abolitionists, who had certainly succeeded
in working up the feelings of the North to a lively pitch of
excitement on Southern Slavery. They were not, of course,
disposed to borrow the extreme views of these zealots, which
were wholly incompatible with the existence of the Union;
but they thought they might venture to utilize to their advan-

tage the Anti-slavery sentiments that had been so skilfully aroused. They set about this very adroitly by raising a cry against extending ·slave territory, which, it was supposed, would please the susceptibilities of the North and not too much exasperate the South. Thus we find that eminent politician, Mr. Seward, already at work in 1850, sowing the seeds of the new Anti-slavery party of the North, by opposing the healing policy of Mr. Clay, on the ground of its fostering slavery and increasing its area.

One of the prominent measures of the Compromise of 1850, was the new Fugitive Slave Law, which Daniel Webster declared to be far more favorable to the Blacks than that recommended by Washington, in 1787. Yet it was seized upon by the cunning of the Anti-slavery politicians to keep up the subsiding agitation, and several of the Legislatures of the Northern States were induced to pass "Personal Liberty Bills," in imitation of the example set by Massachusetts.

I must not omit to remark that the Abolitionists still kept on the even tenor of their way, and were as active as ever in promulgating their impracticable theory by secretly circulating tracts, books, and pictures, harping on slavery and all its fancied horrors. They still kept possession of the political field, and still hoped to make a ladder of their hobby by which to ascend to power. In 1852, they dropped Mr. Birney, and selected for their Presidential candidate Mr. Hale, of New Hampshire. He received 157,000 votes, against the 7,000 thrown for Birney, in 1840.

Among other ingenious modes of excitement, a discussion was regularly kept alive at the North as to the citizenship of free Blacks. Several States bestowed the suffrage upon them, as a practical proof of their right to rank as citizens. This controversy was rather inflamed than otherwise, by a decision of the Federal Supreme Court, in the Dred Scott case, 1853, which settled that no Blacks are citizens of the United States. In 1854, the Slavery question reappeared in Congress, and the action of the North and South on this occasion was pregnant with serious consequences. Two new territories of the West were pronounced sufficiently occupied to render legislation necessary, and a bill to create a territorial government in Kansas and Nebraska, was reported by Mr. Douglas, of Illinois. His bill contained a clause to repeal the famous Missouri line of 36° 30', running south of the territories in question. This line was the basis of compromise in 1820, and was again a means of adjusting the dispute that arose on the admission of Texas, in 1845. The constitutionality of this line was, however, more than doubtful, for the reason that Congress never had any power conferred on it by the Constitution to legislate on slavery; nor was it at all necessary, since individual States could retain or exclude slavery, according to their pleasure. Besides, the line in question was really a nullity, because slavery was so unprofitable to the north of it that it would never be carried there. It was only to the south of this line that the cotton culture made slavery a profit and a necessity. Hence the South made no objection to its repeal, in 1854; but it is difficult to perceive what motive Mr. Douglas could have had in proposing this repeal, unless it was merely to fan the glowing embers of the Slavery question.

No sooner was this Missouri line revoked, than a prompt and significant movement was made in the New England States. Emigrant Aid Societies were formed, as already mentioned; and settlers for Kansas, one of the territories just organized, were lustily summoned as recruits in the new crusade against slavery, and funds in the way of bounty were liberally distributed. This unusual means to stimulate emigration was designed to secure Kansas as a Free State, by obtaining a majority for the Northern people. Such an attempt, made with demonstrations of vehement hostility to the South, was sure to provoke anger and resistance. This, of course, was calculated upon by the Anti-slavery propaganda, and they were not disappointed. The Slave State of Missouri, directly adjoining Kansas, was not disposed to be forestalled, and, as it were, forced out of their legal share to territory in such close proximity; so they did their best to encourage emigration too, but the Slaveholders were naturally chary to carry their Blacks with them, as they were sure to be tempted away. As a matter of course, it was impossible for the people of the two opposite sections, in their intemperate state of mind, to live long in peace together. Collisions occurred, and occasional loss of life ensued. The Abolitionists were eagerly waiting for some such news as this, for it was rightly anticipated that a conflict, sooner or later, was inevitable.

When the looked-for intelligence at last arrived, a wild and furious shriek for "bleeding Kansas" vibrated in a thousand echoes through all the valleys of New England. The organs of the Abolitionists teemed with the most discordant appeals to the passions of the people, and nothing but imprecations of the most startling description were launched against the "Border Ruffians," as the settlers from Missouri were forthwith christened. Public meetings were called in the Eastern States, and the Pulpit soon became a rostrum for clerical agitators. Subscriptions were rapidly set on foot to buy arms and ammunition for the sacred defenders of Anti-slavery in Kansas, whose brows were encircled with the halo of martyrdom. Speculators in "Sharpe's rifles" joined in the well-sustained chorus of the Abolitionists, and a considerable profit was the result. At a public meeting in New Haven, a well-known Abolitionist, Rev. H. Ward Beecher, of Brooklyn, and brother of the authoress of "Uncle Tom's Cabin," aided by his presence and language to swell the clamor fast rising in the North. He desired his name to be subscribed for "twenty-five Sharpe's rifles," and announced he would collect the money to pay for them in his church the following Sabbath, which was done.

Your Lordship may readily infer that such ingenious modes as these, and so skilfully handled, could not fail to excite the sympathies and stir the passions of any community. Ever since 1828, the Abolition party had been laboriously engaged in sapping the mind of the North on the subject of Black Slavery; nor must it be forgotten that they appealed to something more than its philanthropy, when they raised the cry of "No more Slave Territory," which simply meant that all that vast extent of country stretching from the Mississippi to the

Rocky Mountains, should be given up to Northern emigration. It was natural, certainly, that so palatable a doctrine should be acceptable at the North; but just as natural that it should be unwelcome at the South, whose equal claims were so unceremoniously ignored.

The harvest so industriously tilled by the Abolitionists, was now ripe; and the leaders of the old Whig, or Northern party, experienced, astute, and with an organization extending over the entire North, stepped forward, and brushing from their path the noisy fanatics who had sown the seed, they gathered for their own garners the luxuriant crop of Anti-slavery sentiment now sprouting all over the North. They met in convention in Philadelphia, June, 1856, and unfurling the flag of the "Republican Party," made, for the first time, a sectional issue the basis of party action. They selected for their Presidential candidate Mr. John C. Fremont, most reputably known in the country as an officer of the army, but without any political antecedents. It was thought judicious not to nominate a politician too closely identified with the Anti-slavery movement, lest the possible consequences might alarm the "sober second thought" of the North. Thus accoutred, the Republican party went to the polls, November, 1856, and brought off a vote of 1,334,558. They were defeated by the Democratic party, which was now the only link between North and South; but the Republican leaders felt quite sanguine that, with the tactics their experience would suggest, they would carry off the Presidential prize in 1860. It was thus that the moral question as to the sin of slavery, borrowed from England by our Abolitionists, and kept alive by their address till the North was thoroughly infected by it, was, at last, converted into a political question and made a party issue.

It is hardly necessary to hint to a veteran like your Lordship, that the Republican politicians had not the remotest idea of interfering with slavery, if they could help it; but they, doubtless, felt a dread lest the Northern masses, who had conscientiously imbibed the Anti-slavery poison, might force them reluctantly to carry their unconstitutional theories into legislation. It is certain they had their misgivings, but there was no alternative. Without a principle or a measure to brandish against their political opponents, there was nothing but to abandon the hope of office, or to do battle with the dangerous arm they had taken from the hands of the Abolitionists. Unfortunately, ambition outweighed patriotism ; and during the four years just elapsed, the country has been distracted with the din of the Anti-slavery propaganda. Orators, writers, lecturers, and preachers have all joined in the *mêlée*, and their united efforts were directed to the apotheosis of the Negro and the excommunication of the luckless Slaveholder. Every church, public hall, and hustings through the North, has rung with anathemas against the vilified South ; and it is not strange, therefore, that people accustomed to this unbroken strain of vituperation, should begin to believe, at last, that slavery was quite as hideous as it was painted.

In October, 1859, an event occurred which amazed the whole country. I allude to the invasion of the State of Virginia by John Brown and his retinue of a dozen men, which, doubtless, your Lordship remembers. This man Brown, it appears, had figured in "bleeding Kansas" as a daring ringleader of the Anti-slavery bands that had contended for the mastery there. When these bloody contests subsided, he was reduced to inaction ; and he chafed at the loss of the stern excitement congenial to his fierce nature. Whether it was fanaticism, or ambition that inspired him, no one can say ; but he conceived the horrible project of setting on foot a servile insurrection that would, if successful, have given the whole South up to rapine and murder. Followed by a handful of desperate men, he suddenly entered the State of Virginia, seized the arsenal of the Federal Government to obtain the arms he needed, and raised the cry of "Freedom to Slaves." To his astonishment, no doubt, the affrighted Blacks ran to their masters for protection, and some were shot in seeking to escape. This nefarious attempt was quelled by the arrest of Brown and his confederates, and their subsequent trial and execution.

One thing was proved by the utter failure of this daring

outrage, for it showed that the Blacks were contented with their homes, and desired not the emancipation of the sword. Another thing, if not quite so clear, at least looked ominous. This madman, Brown, had been known as an efficient instrument in the hands of the Anti-slavery party of New England; and it was, therefore, a matter of conjecture at the South how far he was incited to this fearful attempt against their very existence. Had they not some reason to think the act met the approval of the Abolitionists of the North, when 300 bells tolled for the fate of Brown, and when the organs of the party honored his memory while affecting to disapprove his conduct?

Your Lordship can readily imagine this event sank deep into the mind and heart of the Southern States. They were led to believe, for the first time, that the ultra wing of the Republican party contemplated the confiscation of their property and the destruction of their lives.

While a prey to these sad forebodings, another incident occurred in the summer of 1860, which deepened their conviction that the Northern States had entered into a dark conspiracy to desolate their land with fire and sword. It was discovered that a book, called the "Impending Crisis," was being secretly circulated all over the North as a "campaign document," a name given here to publications used in a Presidential canvass. The purport of this volume was to show, by assertion, as well as by figures, that the free labor of the North was more profitable than the Black labor of the South. This was a fair topic of discussion, but the tone of the book was violent in the extreme. I will add a few extracts, which will enable your Lordship to form a correct opinion of the character and object of the work:

"Slavery is a great moral, social, civil, and political evil, to be got rid of at the earliest practical period"—(page 168).

"Three-quarters of a century hence, if the South retains slavery, which God forbid! she will be to the North what Poland is to Russia, Cuba to Spain, and Ireland to England"—(p. 163).

"On our banner is inscribed—No Co-operation with Slaveholders in Politics; no Fellowship with them in Religion; no Affiliation with them in Society. No Recognition of Pro-slavery men, except as Ruffians, Outlaws, and Criminals"—(p. 156).

"We believe it is, as it ought to be, the desire, the determination, and the destiny of the Republican party to give the death-blow to slavery"—(p. 234).

"In any event, come what will, transpire what may, the institution of slavery must be abolished"—(p. 180).

"We are determined to abolish slavery at all hazards—in defiance of all the opposition, of whatever nature, it is possible for the Slavocrats to bring against us. Of this they may take due notice, and govern themselves accordingly"—(p. 149).

"It is our honest conviction that all the Pro-slavery Slaveholders deserve to be at once reduced to a parallel with the basest criminals that lie fettered within the cells of our public prisons"—(p. 158).

"Shall we pat the bloodhounds of slavery? shall we fee the curs of slavery? shall we pay the whelps of slavery? No, never"—(p. 329).

"Our purpose is as firmly fixed as the eternal pillars of heaven; we have determined to abolish slavery, and so help us God! abolish it we will"—(p. 187).

The volume containing the above quotations, not by any means the most bitter, was indorsed by 68 members of Congress of the Republican party, whose names were given for publication. I think your Lordship will hardly be surprised if the South, under manifestations like these, exhibited no small alarm. They felt they had a right to infer that, if a party making such declarations of hostility were elected to power by the North, they must either consent to the early abolition of Black Slavery, or retain it by seceding from the Union.

When the British Government emancipated the Blacks in her colonies, she acted with the strictest commercial equity; but the book in question repudiates any compensation to the "curs and whelps of slavery." One more extract:

"The black god of slavery which the South has worshipped for 237 years"—(p. 163).

Now, the writer is ignorant that the South protested for years, first, against the Mother Country, and, next, against New England, importing slaves within her borders. However, the object of the book was to inflame the mind of the North against the South, and therefore falsehood was just as good as truth.

In April, 1860, the delegates of the Democratic party met in convention at Charleston, South Carolina, to make their nomination for the Presidency. The Northern wing of the party proposed Senator Douglas as the most eligible candidate at the North, from his doctrine of "Popular Sovereignty."* The Southern wing objected, as they considered said doctrine only a concession to the Anti-slavery dogma. Mr. Douglas, unhappily, did not withdraw his name, and a rupture of the party ensued. The Northern delegates nominated Mr. Douglas, in Baltimore, June 18; and on the same occasion the Southern delegates nominated Vice-President Breckinridge.

This unfortunate schism doubled the chances of the Republican party, which met in convention to select their candidate at Chicago, Illinois, May, 1860. It was generally supposed that Mr. W. H. Seward, the acknowledged leader of the Anti-slavery party at the North, an able and accomplished statesman, would be its chosen champion in the electoral lists about to open; but, to the surprise of all, an almost unknown politician of the West, Mr. Abraham Lincoln, was selected as its standard-bearer.

It would be no easy matter to explain to your Lordship why the founder and foremost man of a party in this country should, on a supreme occasion like this, be thrown aside and another exalted over his head, with no apparent claim to so great a distinction. It seems to have become almost a rule, of late years, to exclude the leading men of either party from the candidateship to the Presidency. This is a strange enigma, and can lead to no good. Expediency is the pretext. It is alleged, as one reason, that a prominent man offers too broad a target to the opposition Press; but the truth probably is, that the ablest men are likely to be less pliant than obscure politicians, in the hands of those party managers who control nominations in this country, from the President down to a tide-waiter.

On the 6th of November, 1860, the long struggle between the North and South on the slavery question, that began in 1803, ended with the election to the Presidency of Abraham

---

* Mr. Douglas proposed giving the people of a Territory the right to retain or exclude slavery, instead of reserving the decision till the Territory was admitted as a State, the practice hitherto.

Lincoln, the representative of the Republican party, but which contained within its bowels, like the Trojan horse of old, the armed men of the Abolition party. Shortly after this event, Governor Andrew, of Massachusetts, declared at a public meeting, that "the election of Mr. Lincoln was only the first step towards forcible emancipation."

The advent of the Anti-slavery party to power, filled the Southern States with dismay. It mattered little to them whether the Republican party could control the Abolitionists, or whether the latter could dominate the former. It mattered little whether the Anti-slavery President was supported or not by majorities in both Houses of Congress. What they saw, felt, and comprehended in this election, was the fatal fact that the North had pronounced against the institution of Black Slavery. Whether it was meant to limit it, or abolish it, they knew not; but it was clear to them they must prepare for either, if they remained any longer members of the Confederacy.

Whether this logic is well-founded; whether the South should have abided more aggression; whether fear has overcome judgment, or whether fury courts open hostility, I know not; but the South has thrown herself into the arms of Secession with a wild *abandon*, which shows that passion has seized on every fibre of her frame.

The country is in the jaws of a fearful crisis. A miracle alone can save it. It reminds me of the condition of France in the autumn of 1851. The politicians of the Monarchical and Republican parties were fiercely struggling against each other for power, while the country was rapidly drifting towards anarchy. It was useless to reason with either. The Republicans told you they would obtain power first; and the Monarchists, with a grim smile, asseverated they would obtain it at last. It was the sublime courage of Louis Napoleon that saved the State from countless calamities. He boldly closed the doors of the Assembly on the indecent strife of these selfish brawlers, and appealed to the people of France. Millions of voices rent the air with applause; millions of votes sanctified the heroic act.

Our destiny is still a problem, my Lord. Are we utterly at the mercy of those politicians who are ready to sacrifice the national good for their personal interest?—a class of men the poet has stigmatized—

"Flectere si nequeo Superos, Acheronta movebo."

Have we no patriots? Are the people helpless? Must we die on our own swords, amid the derision of Europe?

These are poignant questions, my Lord, and, to our humiliation, no response can be given.

RÉSUMÉ.

The whole territory of the United States was originally slaveholding—English, Spanish, and French. Not from any local law, but from the laws of the mother country.

Slaves were regarded only as property in all the thirteen States that formed the Union; since it would have been a manifest absurdity for the Slaveholders who made the Declaration of Independence, to declare "all men were born free and equal," had they not considered their slaves as property.

In forming the Union, the thirteen Slave States conferred upon the Federal Government the power to tax slave property; to protect it from foreigners, as well on the national territories as at sea, and also from domestic escape; and conferred no other power, either to prohibit or to extend it.

Opinions on slavery varied with its profits. The South repelled it when it was not profitable, and adhered to it when cotton made it so. The North clung to the profits of the Slave Trade as long as possible, and attacked the slave system when they were deprived of those profits.

The territory that was once all slave, has become free;—1st, by the Ordinance of 1787, prohibiting slaves north of the Ohio; 2d, by eight Northern States abolishing slavery in their borders; 3d, by the Missouri Compromise of 1820, prohibiting slaves north of 36° 30'; 4th, the act admitting Texas re-enacting that line. Thus the North has driven slaves out of half the territories of the United States, showing a constant and large aggression upon the South.

The duty of the Government is undoubtedly to protect the property upon the Territories, until people there settled form their own laws.

The agitation of the Slave question grew originally out of the chagrin of New England, at being deprived of the Slave Trade and its profits. It was prolonged by the mutual irritation that the opposition of Massachusetts to the purchase of Louisiana occasioned.

Emancipation made steady progress in all the States, until Abolition forced the Slaveholders upon the defensive.

Abolition made little progress, until unscrupulous partisans coquetted with it for party issues.

The question of the power of the Government to exclude slavery from the Territories, has been blended with the moral question as to the "sin of slavery."

The cry of "Free Soil" was raised in 1848, by Mr. Van Buren, to avenge his non-nomination by the South, at Baltimore.

The compromise measures of 1850, were carried by the influence of Henry Clay.

Violation of these compromises, by the "Personal Liberty Bills" of the Northern States, soon followed.

Repeal of the "Missouri Compromise," in 1854, with support of the South.

Attempt, by the Abolition party, to make Kansas a Free State by force, which was resisted by the South.

Rise of Republican party under the lead of Mr. W. H. Seward, and its defeat in 1856.

Violent agitation of the Slavery question at the North, followed by the invasion of Virginia by John Brown, in 1859, and the secret circulation of the Helper Book, in 1860.

Excessive alarm and exasperation of the South.

The theory of a "Higher Law" at the North, to justify resistance to the Constitution and laws of Congress, has begotten the Higher Law of Self-preservation at the South, to justify resistance to a dominant party which embraces the "sin of slavery" among its tenets.

COMMENTARY.

Before dropping the subject of Slavery in the United States, it is proper, my Lord. I should make known the sentiments of the moderate men of this country on the extraordinary fact that England should have assumed the foremost rank in the anti-slavery crusade against our Southern States. They recollect that England introduced slavery into this country. They remember she upheld it against the remonstrances of the Southern Colonies. They know that England only abandoned it when no longer profitable. They think it, therefore, unreasonable that England should turn her back on these glaring facts; and they feel that in face of them, it is unjust and indecent for Englishmen to give way to denunciation of slavery and abuse of Slaveholders.

It is difficult, my Lord, for them to suppress their indignation at the torrents of invective incessantly launched by England against slavery in the United States, when they reflect that but for the manufacturers of Manchester, African slavery would long since have died out in this divided land. It seems to every honest and practical mind in this country, that upon this subject, England is guilty of the most transparent hypocrisy. If she conscientiously abhors the institution, why does she consume its products? If she cannot exist without them, why then assail the slave-labor that yields them?

It is time, my Lord, and the present crisis proves it, that the Statesmen and Press of England should pause and reflect solemnly on conduct both inconsistent and puerile. It is a matter that must no longer be left to fanatics, else the consequence to England will be serious indeed. It is a topic that must be calmly argued and practically treated. What, then, will be the result? Why, such a revolution of opinion in England as the world has rarely witnessed. When once it becomes known there, and full soon it must, that the emancipation of our Blacks would reduce the cotton crop one-half, and double the price of the remainder; that, in consequence, the manufactures of England would lose their ascendency in the markets of the world, involving the loss of countless millions—who can doubt but that a people so intelligent and practical as the English, would be terror-struck at facts so formidable and incontestable? But when it became further known, and investigation will make it clear, that all the thrilling books and sentimental stories, that all the eloquent essays and speeches from the pen of a Macaulay and the lips of a Brougham, are little else than extravagant rhapsodies; that the condition of our Blacks has been misrepresented, their wrongs invented, and their sufferings imagined;—when calumnies and exaggerations like these, I say, are swept away,—and the event is near at hand,—what, my Lord, will be the force of the reaction that must inevitably follow? For the sake of England, whose interests are in danger; for the sake of this country, whose prosperity is menaced, I trust that facts and reason will be invoked when African Slavery in the United States is henceforth discussed, and that mock appeals to a mistaken humanity will be discarded.

I should weary your Lordship's attention, were I to attempt to enumerate a tithe of the idle stories that have circulated in the British Press, disparaging the happy condition of our Blacks. How many tears have been shed by the credulous; how many sensitive hearts have throbbed in vain over cruelties and horrors that never existed! It is but a short time, for instance, since the English journals gave wide currency to a graphic recital of scenes of violence and deeds of barbarity that almost froze the blood of every reader. Yet it turned out that this heart-rending tale was a miserable hoax, and that its credulous author, John Arrowsmith, a cotton-broker of Liverpool, while travelling in our Southern States, had fallen a victim to the waggish propensities of some of his fellow-travellers, who had discovered his sentimental weakness on the subject of slavery. To this day, however, no contradiction of this fiction has ever appeared.

Again, it was but the other day, that the English journals
teemed with the details of a brutal outrage on the Prince of
Wales, in Richmond, the capital of Virginia. Yet, upon the
high authority of the Duke of Newcastle, nothing of the kind
ever happened, and the story was only an invention of our
Abolition Press to excite the hatred of the loyal English
against our Southern States.

Such are the odious tactics that have been for years employed by the Abolition party in England and the United
States, to sow the seeds of that catastrophe now impending in
the disunion of this Confederacy, entailing, perchance, the
downfall of British manufactures.

As one mode of arresting this calamity, let the public men
of England hereafter admit that with the emancipation of our
Blacks, they have nothing whatever to do. Let them honestly
avow that any aspersion of the domestic institutions of our
Southern States, is an unjust and presumptuous interference
with others' affairs. The immediate effect of this would be to
check the rant and dampen the ardor of the Abolition party
among us.

You can little imagine, my Lord, the immense *prestige* of
the great names of England in this country; nor is it possible
to measure the extent of their influence and the force of their
example. This doctrine of Abolition, which inspires so many
of our politicians, moralists, and preachers, has been transplant-
ed, as I have shown, from England; and its currency here is not
due to its intrinsic merits, but to the high and sounding titles
that have indorsed it. If this be doubted, let the experiment
be tried. Let this insane crusade against our Southern States
be frowned upon by Englishmen of rank and sense; let the
London Times direct its thunderbolts against the pigmy imita-
tors of your noble fanatics; let titled ladies of the "West-End"
no longer lionize the cringing writers and orators of our New
England school—the descendants in blood and doctrine of
those very Puritans who, I repeat, threw England into anarchy, proscribed her nobility, and beheaded her unfortunate
king. Let this be done, my Lord, and the impracticable Abo-

lition party of this country will soon draw its last breath. Let this be done, and the South will be conciliated, and the North will be sobered. Let this be done, and the Union of these States may be prolonged, the manufacturing industry of England be preserved, and, above all, the condition of our Southern Blacks be mitigated or improved, if need there be of either.

I shall forbear, my Lord, from entering into any minute details on the condition, moral or physical, of our Southern Blacks; though much, indeed, might be said and proved of both, that would dispel the ignorance and mitigate the prejudice of the really humane.

If the *Times* newspaper of London would but send one of its accomplished and impartial correspondents to report on the character of Black Slavery in our Southern States, depend upon it, my Lord, the artillery of Exeter Hall would be forever silenced. Despairing of such a consummation, I will limit myself to a brief quotation from the columns of a Northern journal, which my own observation enables me to assert is only a fair and truthful portrait of Negro life at the South:

" Compared with European laborers, the Black lives like a prince. He has his cabin generally neat and clean, and always weather-proof. He has likewise his own garden-patch, over which he is lord paramount. He is *well fed, well lodged, well clothed, and never overworked.* His holidays are numerous, and enjoyed with infinite gusto. Sleek, happy, and contented, the Black lives to a great age. The Slaveholder finds it *to his interest* to treat his Negroes liberally, and takes every means to make them healthy and contented."

In striking confirmation of the above, I extract from the mortuary records of the last year the following cases of Negro slaves who lived to over a hundred years:

1860—February 2	......	Female slave	.... Virginia	 105
....— "	15	...... Milly Lamar	.... Georgia	 135
....—March	25	...... Sam	.... "	 140
....—April	17	...... Glasgow	.... Kentucky	 112

I submit, my Lord, that such extraordinary instances of longevity are conclusive as to adequate nourishment and moderate labor.*

In fine, my Lord, I consider it only fair and reasonable for us Americans, who have been obliged for years to bear inordinate opprobrium at the hands of your canting Abolitionists, to indulge occasionally in a *tu quoque.* Some late English journals furnish incidents it is impossible to resist quoting, since they so forcibly and painfully illustrate the contrast between slave-life in our country, and peasant-life in your Lordship's. I make these quotations, not from any vindictive or uncharitable feeling, but in the earnest hope that foreign criticism may stimulate English people to look at home, and not waste all their humanity in lamentations over our Blacks, while such shocking wretchedness haunts the hovels of their own color and kind.

[From the *Liverpool Post*, December 11.]

"In the London *Times* of yesterday, Mr. Henry Tucker, magistrate of the county of Berks, publishes a document which is quite pitiable enough to fill the nation with horror and reproach. The song of the 'Happy Homes of England' can no longer be sung except as a fiction, for the rural districts afford specimens in abundance of the unhappy homes of England.

"Mr. Tucker employed two competent persons to obtain correct information respecting the condition of the rural cottages, and he laid the result before the meeting of the Farringdon Agricultural Library on the 22d of last month. In doing this he expressed his belief that the condition of Farringdon Union is only a sample of the agricultural population of England. 'Indeed,' he says, 'I have been assured by farmers that the want of decent accommodation has for some time past been driving the superior class of peasantry to emigrate; and that unless some reformation be brought about,

* As a *pendant* to slave-life painted by novelists, I append an extract from the Sermon, already noticed, of Rev. Dr. N. Adams, at Boston, on Jan. 4, 1861:

"There are pictures of loving-kindness in the daily history of those masters and mistresses, the contemplation of which will, by and by, change our tone of feeling towards them, and make us inquirers and learners, and not dictators on this subject. To illustrate my remark: A Northern lady in the South called upon a Southern lady, and found her nursing a black infant. It was the infant of one of her servants. The child was sick, and it died upon the lap of the mistress; the slave-mother could not nurse the child; her mistress did it for her. That mistress was the sister of a Vice-president of the United States. That is 'slavery;' yes, it is as truly 'slavery' as 'auction blocks' are slavery. Yes, we may look for the time, not far off, when Christians at the South will come to be regarded by our people to be as humane and benevolent as they."

none but the feeble and most ignorant will remain in places where decent lodging is not to be procured.' We subjoin a few of the items in the 'Digest:'—

"WOOLSTONE. — Man and wife, two grown-up sons, and an illegitimate child of the daughter, all sleep in one room; man and wife, with a son and two daughters, sleep in one room; two married couples and a child sleep in one room; man and wife, with daughter and two sons, sleep in one room.

"WATCHFIELD.—A father and three daughters sleep in one room on ground floor; seven persons, in a two-roomed cottage, of whom two are lodgers, sleeping in the pantry; a father sleeping with his daughter, seventeen years of age, and the wife in another bed.

"LONGCOT.—Man and wife with a child, one widower and one single woman with a child, making six persons, sleeping in one room: two daughters, each with an illegitimate child; a son, aged twenty, co-habiting with a woman, and four other persons, making ten in one room, with two beds.

"FERNHAM.—Eleven persons sleeping in two bedrooms, both on the ground floor; seven persons do.; ten persons do.; son and daughter, over sixteen years of age, with two other persons, sleeping in one room: three sons and a daughter, and two younger children, with father and mother, sleeping in a room eight by twelve feet; two single men lodging with a man and wife, with four children, making eight persons sleeping in one room; two brothers and two sisters, above sixteen years of age, with father, mother, and four children, making ten persons sleeping in one room.

"FARRINGDON.—Sixteen cottages in Red row. This is stated to be the most wretched place the reporter ever saw. Nine cot-

tages lately indicted for a nuisance, but still very bad. In one cottage the drain flows into the sitting-room, and in another the drain at front door is offensive. Three cottages are badly off for water. Several cottages in a bad state of drainage.

"LECHLADE.—A man and wife, with a female lodger and five children, sleeping 'pell mell' together.

"BUCKLAND.—A man and wife, with two grown-up girls and two other children, all sleeping in one room: a man and wife, with four children, including a grown-up girl, all sleep in one room; a widow, with grown-up son and daughter, and a lodger, all sleep in one room; a woman slept for a long time with a son aged twenty-four.

"LONGWORTH.—Most of the cottages in this village are very old, some of them scarcely fit to live in. (Said to be ecclesiastical property.)

"KINGSTON LISLE.—Most of the cottages have only one small bedroom, yet the families are large, and the majority take lodgers. Example—Man and wife, with five children, and two men and three women lodgers, making twelve persons sleeping in one room.

"BALKING.—Man and wife, with grown-up daughter and son, and four illegitimate children of daughter, all sleep in one small room.

"STANFORD.—A son over 16 years sleeps with father and mother. Four wretched tenements, with only one sleeping-room to each, occupied by large families. Of another it is said, 'a regular sty, not fit for human beings to live in,' yet seven persons live and sleep in the same room.

"'In addition,' says Mr. Tucker, 'to this degraded and degrading state of the agricultural laborers of England, as regards domestic comfort, many of the villages are reported as having no school, and hence ignorance and vice go hand in hand, and no exertion appears to be made to check the demoralization of so large a portion of the community. Surely, sir, the act of Parliament which authorizes the government to advance money to landed proprietors for the draining of land, erecting farm-buildings, &c., might extend its provisions to the more important duty of housing the poor, if it were only with even half the comfort in which we house our cattle and our horses.'"

I must confess my astonishment, my Lord, that misery and destitution like this is allowed to exist a single hour in England, which is not only the richest country in the world, but I believe from long observation to be the most charitable. The enormous sums annually collected in England by missionary and eleemosynary societies of all kinds, would convert every English peasant into something like a millionaire. Surely this is a case, if ever there were one, to apply the familiar saying, that " charity should begin at home."

Why do not the humanity-mongers of Exeter Hall withdraw for a while their fascinated gaze from the shining faces of our merry Blacks, to the contemplation of the hollow cheeks and emaciated frames of their own fellow-countrymen? Let them vindicate the fame of England from the foul stigma of such squalor as this. Or, if nothing but emancipating slaves will satisfy their rampant ardor; if no home-made poverty, however terrible, can touch the romantic souls of Abolitionists; if they have no delight but in bidding the captive look up and bear himself proudly—

> "Col[u]mque tueri
> Jussus, et erectos ad sidera tollere vultus"—

why, then, let them turn their eyes eastward, and arrest the auctioneer's hammer at Constantinople, which consigns to bondage, not the swarthy, repulsive Negro, but the loveliest specimens of our own race, the fair Circassian; and to what bondage, my Lord?—not the wholesome labor of the cotton-field, but the bestial degradation of the Harem.

THE RESOURCES OF THE SOUTH.

It is not likely that your Lordship has ever had occasion to turn your attention to the natural resources of our Southern States; but, at the present juncture, such an investigation possesses peculiar interest. I shall not venture beyond the most general outline, but shall not fail to say enough to show the immense mutual advantages the two great sections of our country have derived from their commercial union, which abstract questions and idle political contests seem destined to diminish, if not destroy.

The original Colonies of this country were all possessed of slaves, as already stated; and the industry of both sections was nearly the same, since the Imperial Government prohibited manufactures in the Colonies. The North was more commercial; its industry consisted chiefly, as mentioned, in curing and selling fish, and trading largely in Negroes for Southern consumption. The valleys of the Mohawk and the Hudson supplied some farm produce for export; and the South raised, principally, tobacco, indigo, and silk. All these employments were carried on, North and South, by slaves; but none of them were very profitable, since they had but a restricted market for sale, and were obliged to make their purchases of goods from England.

When the present Union was formed, however, a new state of things arose. Manufactures were eagerly embarked in at the North, and the Federal Government adopted such means as it supposed would encourage them. The South continued its usual employments, viz.: the production of raw articles, of which tobacco was the principal, but which rapidly deteriorated the land.

There were in the Southern States, at this period, 657,047 slaves, and at the North, 39,250. The number of the slaves was increasing by importation, while the profits of employing them were diminishing. In 1793, however, the invention of the Cotton-gin, as remarked, changed the face of the future. Up to that time, it required a hand a day to clean one pound of cotton from the seed, for market; but the gin enabled one hand to clean 350 lbs. per day. From that moment the cotton culture began to attract the attention of planters; and up to this day, it has not ceased to increase. The product, in 1800, was 1 bale for 24 slaves, and is now 1¼ bales for 1 slave. At the same time, the value of other articles produced at the South has risen largely. Naval stores, rice, tobacco, and sugar have increased as well as cotton. The value of these five articles produced, in 1800, per head of all the slaves, was $16 per annum; while in the present year it was $67 per head. At the same time, the quantity of food raised on the plantations is also greater. In later years, large planters have raised sufficient nearly to feed their Blacks; while large quantities of food are now exported North. Virginia and Kentucky are the largest corn-growing States of the Union.

When the invention of the Cotton-gin made the culture of that article profitable, it attracted all classes of persons at the South. Retired merchants, professional men, as well as planters, invested in cotton lands, and put all their available means into that culture, which thus absorbed capital from all other pursuits. It followed from this, that the Blacks were concentrated upon the cotton plantations at rising prices, which have gone up from $250 at the beginning of the century, to $1,500 each good field-hand at the present time. It also resulted, from the inordinate pursuit of this single industry, that all others were checked; and as the South increased in numbers and wealth from cotton, it became more and more dependent upon the North for its manufactures and goods. The large market thus offered to Northern industry, was a more effective encouragement to its domestic manufactures than any protective measures the Federal Government could adopt. The North was not, however, contented with that advantage, but insisted upon a monopoly of the supply by an almost prohibitive duty, with a view to exclude English goods. The average, that was 7½ per cent. in 1800, was raised successively in 1816, 1824, and 1828, to 40 per cent. This being found excessive, it was reduced to 25 per cent., at which it continues. This rate is charged upon the proceeds of exports sold abroad, and returning into the country. The exports of merchandise from the United States, in 1859, were as follows:

Merchandise of Southern origin	$198,389,351
" Northern "	78.217,202
Total Merchandise exported	$276,606,553

This large amount, nearly $200,000,000, of Southern produce, may realize abroad, with freights and profits, some $225,000,000, for which goods are taken in return; and the duty of 25 per cent. on these, amounts to $56,000,000, which may be regarded as a bounty on Northern manufactures as against those of England, where the Southern products are mostly sold.

That such a system should build up an immense manufacturing interest at the North, was inevitable. The Federal census of 1850 gave the value of manufactures annually produced, as follows:

	CAPITAL IN MANUFACTURES.	PRODUCTION.
North	$438,249,677	$854,526,679
South	94,995,674	164.579.937
Total Manufactures	$533,245,351	$1,019,106,616

The North also imports for the South, and the value of the whole charged to the South is enhanced in the ratio of the duty, viz., 25 per cent. The North may be said to take all the Southern products, and pay in goods at 25 per cent. advance over the English prices.

The influx of emigrants from abroad, with large capital, aided that development.

The financial operations of the agricultural South, where $300,000,000 worth of crops are annually moved to market, necessarily centred in New York, where the goods are mostly imported and Eastern manufactures are distributed. This fact will serve to explain the annual migration of Southern merchants to the North to make their purchases; and with them often come their families, to visit the fashionable watering-places, where also many of the wealthy Southern planters spend their summers. New York has also become the chief point of connection with Europe, and therefore all Southern travellers come there to embark. These various causes draw a large Southern expenditure to the North, which is not in any way reciprocated.

All the operations of Finance, Banking, Insurance, Brokerage, Commissions, Profits on Imports and on Domestic Manufactures, &c., inure to the North, on the basis of the agriculture of the South. These items have been estimated at an aggregate of $231,000,000 per annum, drawn for Northern account from Southern industry. It is not, therefore, a matter of surprise that the North has accumulated wealth much faster than the South. But it is a matter of surprise that the North, under

these circumstances, should upbraid the South with her comparative poverty.

The North thus reaps the whole of the profits of Slave labor.

I am sure it must strike your Lordship with amazement, that
when the North, by its superior activity and commercial
sagacity, was thus reaping such enormous advantage from the
products of the Slave States of the South, they should allow
themselves to fall a prey to fanatics and excited partisans. An
English statesman, above all others, must be perplexed, and
incredulous of such facts; for, to the eternal honor of British
politics, must it be said that the national good is never for an
instant endangered by schemes of personal aggrandizement.

The result of these constant attacks of Northern fanaticism,
have not only irritated the South, but forced them to pay more
attention to their interest than heretofore. They begin to feel
a desire to keep at home at least a portion of the capital produced there, and with it employ the poorer white population
of the " Border States," where Slave labor is not profitable,
since it is not a cotton region. They are disposed, of late, to
commence developing those manufactures for which they have
hitherto been dependent on the North.

The North takes of the South 750,000 bales of cotton, worth
$50,000,000, per annum; which it works up into cotton goods,
to send back to the South. That quantity of cotton will make
1,035,000,000 yards of cotton cloth, for which $100,000,000
is charged; but England will sell the same quantity for
$75,000,000, and if the South makes it herself, it may be done
for $60,000,000. Southern economists see that to make this
great saving, nothing else is necessary than to keep at home
the capital now drained off to the North. The Abolitionists of
New England have driven the South into these calculations,
and thus it is her own children conspiring her ruin.

One word more of the self-sustaining resources of the South,
which I extract from a Northern journal. I give 't without
comment.

"The Southern States, including Virginia, Kentucky, Georgia, Tennessee,
North Carolina, and most of South Carolina, are the finest grain-growing

conntries in the world; and were not cotton, tobacco, and rice more profitable, those States might export corn, wheat, and other cereals in large quantities. The slopes of the Alleghanies on both sides are as fertile and as well suited for the production of breadstuffs of all kinds, as any lands in the conntry. They are covered with beantiful farms, the soil and the climate are alike favorable, and it is the height of absurdity to talk of the poverty of the Sonthern States. To some extent at present they cultivate other crops, which they exchange for food, because they can do so with advantage to themselves; but throw them on their own resources, and cut them off from Northern and Western supplies, and they can produce not only enough for themselves, but compete with the North in exportation, to the serious damage of its interests.

"In the interior of the Sonthern States almost every description of food abounds, and is far cheaper than in the Northern and Eastern States. It is only a strip of the seaboard that forms the exception to the rule, and there the production of cotton and rice amply compensates for the deficiency of the cereals. It is only because the conveyance by sea of food to the Southern ports from the North is cheaper than the carriage by railroad from the interior of the Southern States, that wheat, corn, and other grain are shipped to any extent from the North in exchange for cotton, tobacco, and rice. But if the policy of non-intercourse should prevail, the demand at the Southern seaboard would soon produce the necessary supply from the interior. In the event of secession and separate confederacies, however, the North would only be too glad to send its surplus food to the seaports of the South for cash, or for those productions of the South which the North does not yield, and which are better than gold to the Northern States. To use a homely proverb, the North will not always cut off its nose to vex its face, as it is now doing; and the great danger will be, that the South will wholly withdraw its trade and its exchanges from the North, and transfer them to England, France, and other Enropean countries.

"But, after all, it is a very small proportion of the breadstuffs and other food consumed by the Sonthern seaboard that comes from the North. For instance, Mobile derives its chief supplies from New Orleans—one of the cheapest markets in the United States. According to the most recent quotations, the prices at New Orleans, Savannah, Charleston, and New York, compare thus:—

	New Orleans, Nov. 21.		Savannah, Nov. 23.		Charleston, Nov. 23.		New York, Nov. 28.	
Flour.........	$4 50 @	7 50	6 00 @ 7 50		6 00 @	7 50	4 85 @	7 25
Wheat.........	1 25 @	1 60	—		—		1 10 @	1 43
Corn	6¾ @	72	75 @	85	65 @	85	65½ @	6¾
Potatoes......	1 00 @	1 50	1 50	—	1 50 @	2 00	1 50 @	2 00
Bacon	12 @	14	13		12½ @	13	9¼ @	10
Butter.......	10 @	15	15 @	28	15 @	28	14 @	20
Cheese........	9 @	12½	10 @	13	10 @	13	10 @	11
Apples........	1 00 @	3 00	1 00 @ 2 25		—		1 37 @	1 50

"Here, then, it will be seen that the average cost of these essential articles of food, is less at New Orleans than it is at New York; and from New Orleans, which is supplied by the Mississippi, all parts of the cotton Gulf States are accessible either by water or by railroad. The Atlantic Cotton States are also connected with the interior Southern States, both by water and railroad communication. At Charleston, it will be observed, corn is nearly as cheap as at New York; and at Savannah, notwithstanding the short crop, owing to drought, the price is very little higher than at the great emporium of the North, where almost daily sales of North Carolina corn and wheat contribute to keep down the prices. Thus the whole argument founded on the power of the North to starve the South, vanishes into thin air, and, 'like the baseless fabric of a vision, leaves not a wreck behind.'

"Then, the South produces food of better quality than the North. Southern flour, for instance, commands the highest price in the market of New York. The average daily sales of Southern flour in this market are from 1,200 to 1,500 barrels; and if we take into account the quantity of flour and other breadstuffs sent here from Virginia, Tennessee, Kentucky, Missouri, North Carolina, and other Slave States, perhaps the balance against the South on the score of food would be exceedingly small.

"The South, moreover, excels the North in its water-power, and teems with coal and other minerals. It has cheaper labor and a better climate, and therefore can successfully compete with the North in manufactures. Owing to the mildness of the weather in winter, its factories can work all the year round; and the South requires less clothing and less fuel for its population (two main items in the expenditure of the Northern mechanic), and therefore a higher degree of comfort can be obtained for the same labor at the South than at the North."

GENERAL VIEW.

THE NORTHERN STATES.

I should but ill discharge the task I have assumed, my Lord, if I did not convey in the most candid language the impressions made upon me by passing events. None but an eye-witness of the struggle that has so suddenly come upon us can form any adequate notion of its extent or duration. • The vital apprehension that becomes more imminent with every succeeding phase of the conflict is, that the Confederacy is in danger. There is no disguising the fact that this sad contingency stares us in the face. It may still be averted, and that solemn responsibility rests upon the States of the North. It is their act that this phantom of Disunion has been conjured up, and upon them alone devolves the effort to exorcise it. Do they appreciate the danger? Alas! I fear not. Do they value the

Union? It is their chief reliance. Why, then, have they staked its existence so wantonly? Allow me to save your Lordship from this prevalent fallacy. In the late Presidential election, the Northern States, it is true, threw their *electoral* vote for the candidate of the Anti-slavery party, but it turns out on analysis that far more than one-half of the popular vote is against him.

It appears that the President elect received but 1,864,000 out of a suffrage of 4,710,548, leaving a balance recorded against him of 2,846,548. It follows, then, from our defective political machinery we shall have a President in office who is the representative of the minority, which is at variance with the very organic law of our institutions, the law of the majority. This incredible fact must absolve a portion of the people of the Northern States from the parricidal folly of seeking to pull down the pillars of their political temple. But I am not the less convinced that the Northern minority who elected. Mr. Lincoln never contemplated for a moment that they were applying a torch to their own dwellings. Their ruling motive was, simply, to give a *congé* to the party in power, who had held it for eight years, and whose term they proposed to terminate. They may have had some vague notions on the subject of slavery. They may have desired not to see it extend into the unsettled Territories, without stopping to reflect what means, if any, could be employed to prevent it. They never imagined, for an instant, that in voting for the " Black Republican" candidate, they were signing the death-warrant of the Confederacy. The proof, my Lord, that I am an honest interpreter of their sentiments will be seen in their future action. When the startling truth breaks upon them that, unconsciously, they have brought the Confederacy to the very verge of an abyss, where revolution and anarchy await them, they will shrink back dumb with amazement and horror. Woe, then, to the false guides who have brought them to such a pass. Upon what data do I found this prediction? First, upon the fact that these people of the North are intelligent and practical; understanding their interests, and cleaving to them at all hazards. Next, their views upon the condition of our Southern Blacks are loose and unsettled. Their feelings have been played upon, but their convictions have not been reached. They will make no sacrifices, therefore, that, on re-flection, achieve no good, and involve enormous loss. Finally, patriotism is not extinct in the heart of the Northern States. "It is not dead, but only sleepeth." A love of our nationality, cemented by the blood of our forefathers, and consecrated by the dying benediction of Washington—*clarum et venerabile nomen*—is still latent in their breasts, and when the occasion comes, will burst forth with electrical effect. Should it turn out otherwise, my Lord,—should these people of the North, reflective, educated, and experienced, wantonly throw into the seething caldron of Revolution the blessings of eighty years of unexampled prosperity,—then may the monarchies of the old world rejoice, for self-government is but a snare and a delusion.

One word more of the Abolition party of the United States. They are really insignificant in numbers, and will be swallowed up in the returning waves of reason. The leaders of this party, who affect to believe in the social and political equality of the White and Black races, are made up of that class who are commonly known as fanatics—a kind of moral lunatics, who strike at all who dispute their grotesque illusions. These worshippers of abstract questions, whom Napoleon stigmatized as "Ideologues," are foes to the peace and welfare of every community, and should be jealously watched and rigidly re-strained. It is an extraordinary fact, and worthy your Lord-ship's attention, that the monopoly of these intellectual fungi is enjoyed by a particular locality in this country, where they seem indigenous to the soil. The State of Massachusetts is not only the head-quarters of Abolition, but it is the hotbed of every kind of chimera in religion, politics, and morals. Can your Lordship credit the fact that a man assuming the title of Reverend* should have devoted every Sabbath in the city of

---

* The late Rev. Theodore Parker.

Boston to blasphemous attacks on the Christian Religion,
while palpitating crowds of men and women flocked after his
sacrilegious eloquence! Is it not equally incredible that a man
of education and fortune,* a citizen of Boston, should habitu-
ally denounce the Constitution of his country, declaring that
it is "a league with hell, and a covenant with death." Not
less marvellous are the attempts so frequently made in Massachusetts to organize "Communities of Free Love," where the
promiscuous intercourse of the sexes is the corner-stone of the
social edifice. If these be the revolting metaphysics of the
Abolitionists of Massachusetts—if this be the religion, the politics, and the morals they would instil into the minds of the
Southern Blacks, far better leave them in harmless ignorance.
That Massachusetts is distinguished by its profound skepticism
of all authority, divine and human, is undeniable, and your
Lordship can hardly imagine the reason assigned for it by the
thinking men among them. They attribute it to EXCESS OF
INTELLECTUAL CULTURE!—which only verifies the saying, that
"human knowledge is the parent of doubt." Let the far-famed
"schoolmaster abroad" resolve this startling problem—that
universal education in Massachusetts has brought forth
Preachers of Infidelity in Religion, Professors of a "Higher
Law" than the Constitution in Politics, and Practical Expo-
nents of the works of St. Simon and Fourier.† This mental
licentiousness was characteristic of the worst period of the first

* Wendell Phillips, Esq.

† In corroboration of the above is the following extract from a Northern journal:

"The people of Massachusetts were very recently warned by one of her own statesmen and orators that 'Yankees are not popular in the Middle any more than in the
Southern States.' He told them that their 'disestimation in the Middle States' was
universal, and assured them that there was 'a project much thought of, as well in the
other non-slaveholding as in the slaveholding States, to reconstitute the Union, ex-
cluding New England from it.' Union men of New England are beginning to hold
up this truth to each other, together with a daguerreotype of the provincial mean-
ness, bigotry, self-conceit, love for 'isms,' hypercritical opposition to any thing and
every thing, universal fault-finding, hard-bargaining, and systematic home lawless-
ness and nullification, while denouncing, as worthy of hanging, counter-nullification
in others, which are covering their section of the country with odium, and creating
the wish elsewhere to relieve the Confederation of the burden by its excision at any
cost."

French Revolution, and is entirely incompatible with good order everywhere.

SOUTHERN STATES.

Before this communication reaches your Lordship, many of our Southern States will have ceased to be members of the late Confederacy, whose brilliant career has inspired so much panegyric, and awakened so many hopes. This solemn event will startle England, and she will deprecate now what only forty years ago she would have rejoiced at. Your Lordship may think the step premature and uncalled-for, but when the facts I have related are properly weighed, the conclusion must be different. The Southern States have been for nearly sixty years the object of political persecution by the North, which they have borne with patience and returned with kindness.* In 1820 the North entered into a compromise, which has been broken. In 1850 they made new agreements, which have since been violated. In 1860 a legal majority elect a President on the " Platform" that " Slavery must be restricted to its present limits." Wounded in their dignity, outraged in their rights, and threatened in their interests, what course is left the South? To fold their arms and await more injury and endure more obloquy? Would this check the aggressions of the North, or only encourage them till both North and South were swallowed up in the same vortex of ruin. It is clear, my Lord, that the South have no alternative. Far better they should abandon the Confederacy than remain only to engage in bitter feuds that compromise the dignity of the country, and sow the seeds of undying hatred.

The secession of the united South will calm the passions of the North and awaken its reason. Reflection will bring repentance, and the South, true to her chivalric nature and generous instincts, will not turn a deaf ear to offers of manly reparation. I, for one, do not despair of such a result.

The right of secession it is idle to discuss with the South.

---

* Witness Mr. Calhoun's conduct in 1816.

In 1789, according to her view, she entered into a civil compact with the North, on certain conditions and guaranties. These have been broken, and the South returns, in her opinion, to her original sovereignty.* Even were it otherwise,—were it true that the South owed allegiance to the Federal government,—still, she asserts, our own Declaration of Independence in 1776, and the present practice of Europe, justify all people in repudiating a government which assails their rights and sacrifices their best interests. If the Northern States do not acknowledge these truths, exclaims the South, then are they false to their origin, and seek to substitute for a government of opinion the tyranny of force. That the South will adhere to its right of secession at all hazards, and at every sacrifice, is clear to me, for her interests demand it. That the North will shrink from an armed attempt to contest it, is equally plain, for her interests forbid it. To suppose that out of deference for a mere abstraction—the exclusive right to savage territories—the Northern States will destroy their commerce, ruin their finances, and desolate their homes, by plunging into the fiery furnace of a civil war, is beyond all imagination. Should this event occur,—should force, and not reason, be the bloody arbitrament in this crisis of our history,—then, I say again, let Despotism hurl its cap in the air, for self-government is only a stupendous sham!

---

* This principle of sovereignty was repeatedly asserted by New England during the last war, and on January 4, 1815, a report of a committee was made in the Hartford Convention, in favor of immediate secession from the Union, on the plea that the Constitution had been violated by the Embargo Act, and the ordering of the militia into the service of the United States. The report defended the right of secession as follows :

"That Acts of Congress, in violation of the Constitution, are *absolutely void*, is an undeniable position. . . . . But in cases of deliberate, dangerous, and palpable infractions of the Constitution, affecting the *sovereignty of a State* and *liberties of the people*, it is not only the *right* but the *duty* of such State to *interpose its authority* for *their protection, in the manner best calculated* to secure that end. When emergencies occur which are either beyond the reach of the judicial tribunals, or *too pressing to admit of the delay incident* to their forms, States *which have no common umpire* must be *their own judges* and *execute their own decisions*. The States should so use their power as effectually to protect their own *sovereignty* and the rights and liberties of their citizens."

But should a war ensue between the North and South, I can foresee no result so certain as the intervention of England, perhaps of France. To both these nations, and especially to the first, is the Southern staple of cotton indispensable. The supply must be steady and full, else the factories of Great Britain would be paralyzed. To save this trade from the eventualities of a civil war, England must interfere either as an umpire or as an ally of the South. The negrophobia of British fanaticism or of British philanthropy will vanish, I venture to predict, before the stern reality of a loss, or even a diminution of the cotton crop. Should the infatuation of the North drive the European Powers to throw the sword of Brennus into the trembling scale, then a Southern Confederacy, with " Free Trade" for its motto, would soon become a *fait accompli*, and the factories of New England would serve but as monuments to record her folly and her ruin.

CONSTITUTIONAL AMENDMENTS.

If my aspirations are realized, my Lord, and the North should manifest a disposition to abandon dogmas and yield to reason, then amendments to our Constitution must follow. The histories of England, the oldest constitutional country of the world, and that of France, furnish ample precedents; but unfortunately in nearly all these cases the blind bigotry of party rendered force the medium of reform.

I cannot but believe that the wisdom of our people will afford a nobler example. Should the revision of our Constitution ensue, the South will demand a final settlement of the Negro question. It will be a happy day for the peace of the country and the condition of the Blacks, when this wearisome dispute is withdrawn forever from the arena of party politics.

Yet, there will still remain other modifications hardly less important. When the present Constitution was adopted, the population of the United States consisted of some four millions, which was pretty equally divided between North and South. Natural increase and immigration have swelled the popular vote of the North so rapidly, that its permanent preponderance over the Federal Government is fully established by the census of 1860. This was never contemplated by the Fathers of the Republic, else it would have been provided for, since nothing is more manifest than their desire to effect a perfect *equality* of the rights and privileges of all the States. It was intended by the Constitution that the South should always have an equal share in the Federal legislation, and that no numerical disparity should confer undue advantage on the North. The purpose of our political architects to preserve equality is shown in the organization of the Senate, where the smallest State of the North wields the same influence with the most populous State of the South.* In the House of Representatives the same just balance was sought.

If from force of circumstances as well as from natural causes the provisions of our early statesmen have failed, and the North have obtained a physical ascendency over the South, it follows that this accidental inequality must be rectified. To desire that the South should deposit forever the Federal government in the hands of the North is unjust. To expect they would consent to do it is absurd. To contend the South has no right to equality in the Federal government is preposterous. To sustain that view by force is tyranny. The Constitution must, then, be modified to suit the new exigencies of our political history, else the South have a double inducement to abandon the Confederacy.

But, should another Constituent Assembly ever meet to readjust our political equilibrium, somewhat disturbed by time and events, many grave questions may be mooted. It is clear that in some essentials our *Magna Charta* was better adapted to our early condition, than now. From a country chiefly agricultural, we have become almost the first manufacturing and commercial nation in the world. These vast interests are the very nerves of every trading community, and are keenly sensitive, as they are vital. Their vigor and growth depend on

* Each State sends two members to the Senate. Each member of the lower house represents the same ratio of population.

the stability of government and the tranquillity of society. It is notorious that our commercial world is seriously disturbed by the frequency of our elections—comprising Municipal, State, and Federal—which involve both disorder and uncertainty. Above all, the Presidential election, coming every four years, and bringing with it, perhaps, an entire change of policy, both domestic and foreign, is found to be more and more detrimental.

From careful observation I should say, my Lord, that if the people of this country, more especially of the North, were to give their conscientious opinion as to the incessant exercise of the elective franchise, they would pronounce it inconvenient and hurtful. The proof of this is the small proportion, in most of our elections, of the vote to the population, which shows indifference to the franchise. The consequence of this neglect is, that our public affairs are falling steadily into the hands of a class of professional politicians, who control the political machine, and work it naturally more for their own advantage than that of the community.* It appears to me that Self-government in the United States at this day, where all, from the lowest to the topmost round, are engaged in lucrative employment, is found to be, in its present form, both troublesome and costly.

* A singular confirmation of this fact is to be found in the new Constitution of the State of New York, which dates from 1846. Among other *reforms* introduced, was that of taking from the Governor the appointment of his Executive Council, such as the Attorney-general, Comptroller of the State, &c., and making these offices elective. The consequence of these officials being independent of the Governor, is not only to render him a nullity, but to divide responsibility, always dangerous. Another result is the probable election of individuals incapable of discharging their functions properly, which could not occur if the Governor were responsible. The object of throwing all these appointments into the hands of the people, however, is achieved; for the embarrassment of a choice is so great that the political managers control the nominations, and put their own men in office. The example set by New York has been imitated, and our new State Constitutions are gradually losing the balance necessary to their preservation. For the first time in history, the statesmen of 1789 succeeded in combining, in wonderful harmony, the three great elements of all perfect political Constitutions, whose especial virtues are *Unity*, *Conservatism*, and *Progress*. By increasing the power of the franchise, our modern tinkerers are destroying the requisite equilibrium, and the consequences must be serious. It was the new Constitution of New York that made the Judiciary elective, a most dangerous innovation.

France has her Self-government. The present Empire is founded on universal suffrage. Yet, rather than have the peace of society compromised by adopting our quadrennial election, and thus disturbing commercial operations, and endangering the precarious gains of the artisan and the operative, the middle and laboring classes of France voted by millions, in 1852, for an Hereditary Executive, a Senate for life, and a House of Representatives (*corps législatif*) for five years. Such institutions guarantee stability, which, in a country so populous as France, is the prime requisite of her active and industrious population.

England has also her form of Self-government, consisting of an Hereditary Executive, an Upper House, also hereditary, and a Lower House for seven years. I consider it no misnomer to apply the term of Self-government to the British system; for the House of Commons is elected by the intelligent middle class—a wise restriction, as we think here—and the Ministry is created, or deposed, solely by the vote of that House, without the co-operation of the co-ordinate branches of the government, viz., the Executive and Upper House. This is virtually Self-government.

Either of these systems has an immense practical advantage over ours, so far as the tranquillity of the community, the security of property, and, above all, the necessities of trade and commerce depend. Such, indeed, are the losses and derangement of business, with us the vital cord, attendant more and more on our Presidential elections, that I do believe, my Lord, if the people of the United States could find a man on whose sense and integrity they might rely, they would gladly elect him for a lengthened period, and rejoice they had escaped the necessity and the risk of exercising the overrated privilege of the franchise. My presumption is, therefore, that in case of a Convention for the amendment of our Federal Chart, efforts will be made, first, to render the President ineligible, and next, to extend his term to eight or ten years. An additional necessity for this is the fact that the Secretaries for the various departments, who come in with the new President, have hardly time, in four years, to know their business, vastly increased since 1789; and, consequently, the Government is too much in the hands of Clerks acquainted with the routine. This might be amended by creating, as in England, permanent Assistant-secretaries of State, more capable and more responsible than simple Clerks.

I doubt not the commercial world, from high to low, would gladly indorse such modifications. It is fast becoming the settled conviction of this country, that the franchise has been forced beyond its true boundary. For instance, an elective Judiciary in several of our States is ruining the Bench, for the ablest lawyers will not abandon their practice for the ermine which may be stripped at any moment from their shoulders. The people besides, it would seem to me, are weary of the incessant demands of the franchise on their time; for, beyond question, they neglect it, while all interested in property and government, as all are in this country, dread its uncertain action more and more.

In short, my Lord, we have experimented in government till all classes begin to feel the necessity of retracing our steps, and of coming back to those limits our sagacious forefathers assigned to us.

THE AMERICAN PRESS.

I have trespassed at such length on your Lordship's attention, that I will limit my concluding remarks to the narrowest space: but I consider it pertinent to glance for a moment at the connection between our Press and the present state of the country. It is thought in Europe, from the freedom of our institutions, that the Press of the United States has an unbounded license and irresistible influence. There is much fallacy in this. Our Press is not under the check of law, as in France, nor of conventional usage, as in England, but the restraint of public opinion here is as stringent as either. It is singular that the character and condition of the Daily Press of the three leading nations of the world should be so unlike. To make myself better understood, may I venture to say a word or two of the French and English Press, however familiar to your Lordship, in order to make the contrast to our own more complete.

In France the Press is a political power; in England, a moral power; in the United States, chiefly, so to speak, a commercial power. In France there are three, if not four, parties struggling against each other for power—two Monarchical, the Legitimist and Orleanist; two Democratic, the Republican and Socialist. The Napoleon Dynasty stands aloof from these, and represents the Nation, its sentiments and interests. Each party has its organs, but the national cause may be said to have no representation in the Press. It is natural that when the prize contended for is the possession of the government, the journals of France should be animated with a boundless ardor. They work with hearty unanimity against the occupant of power, but each hopes, in the scramble, on his overthrow to secure the vacant post. The Press of France is, therefore, more revolutionary than partisan. It was the united Press which undermined the Legitimist throne of Charles X. in 1830, and to the disappointment of many of them, it was the Orleanist branch which carried off the trophy. Again, it was the united Press which sapped the Orleanist Monarchy in 1848, and to the surprise of all of them, the Republican Party sprung into the empty chair. Once more they combined and worked for the restoration of monarchy. It came in 1852, but not the one they had anticipated. It is manifest, then, that the tranquillity of society in France is utterly at the mercy of the Press, whose daily task is to assail the existing Government. It was an immense benefit, therefore, to the trading and commercial interests when Napoleon III. put a check on the excesses of Paris journalism. A free Press in France simply means the privilege of each party to do its best to effect a Revolution. Until these parties and their journals disappear, there is no hope for permanent order. A constitutional government and unrestricted Press, as understood in England and

this country, is impossible for the present in France. The
government of Napoleon has only maintained itself by putting
a muzzle on both the politicians and the journals. Had he
allowed them free scope, he would have been in exile before
this, and France would have lost the vast benefits of his
reign. It has been much the fashion, my Lord, for the English
Press to mourn over the condition of French journalism, and
abuse Napoleon for trammelling it. This must be ignorance
of the stern necessity, or a desire to see France a prey to
anarchy. The Emperor has recently modified his system of
restraint. It is a dangerous experiment, and it will end by attempts against his dynasty, or the cancelling of his concessions.
The greatest French journalist of the day, Emile de Girardin,
once said to me that, " with a single journal, perfectly free, he
could overthrow any government in the world." The remark
is a striking one, and shows that in our day, my Lord, governments, and even society itself, has a new and formidable element to deal with. A mere Party Press like that of France is
any thing but an advantage to the country. It may be regarded, on the other hand, as little less than a nuisance, re-
quiring frequent abatement.

It is no idle compliment to the Press of England to say that
it has raised journalism to the rank it occupies in modern
times. Its consummate ability, its variety of intelligence, and
lofty tone, have together made it not only a lever in politics,
but an arbiter in society. It has come to be not inaptly
termed " the fourth estate of the Realm." It is not so much
in intellect that the English Press surpasses the French, it
strikes me, my Lord, but more in that moderation of opinion
and sobriety of language which imparts force and dignity to
journals as well as men. This may be attributed in some degree to the absence of those fierce party passions which ebb
and flow in France, and also to the salutary influence of the
Aristocracy on manners, but more than all to the character of
the people themselves, which is not mercurial like the French,
nor impulsive like the American, but subdued and reserved.
It follows, then, that a journal which aspires to influence or

profit in England, must be what is there called "respectable:" that is, scrupulous in its statements and careful in its language. During nearly the whole of this century the journalism of England has been of a partisan character, and has been divided in its support of one or the other of the two great parties, Whig and Tory, into which the Aristocracy was ranged. Thus, the Tory Press has maintained the prerogatives of government, while the Whig journals have contended for an increase of popular liberty. In the course of years it came to pass that the Tory party, having yielded every thing, disappeared altogether; while the Whig party, having gained every thing, likewise disappeared. It seems to me, that at the present day political parties have ceased to exist in England for want of a pretext. The Aristocracy are ready to concede every rational demand, while the Middle Class, which regulates the Lower Class, appears to have nothing to ask. The consequence is, the Press has been obliged to find other interests to represent, and it has become in a great degree a class Press, addressed to the pursuits and tastes of various classes and callings. The great champions of Whig and Tory principles have either vanished entirely, or shrunk into small proportions; while the community is deluged with journals—Literary, Medical, Legal, Clerical, Artistic, and Scientific, to say nothing of the Illustrated tribe which caters for the sense as well as the mind.

From the decadence of party organs in England has arisen a new and commanding feature of journalism, the Independent Press. This modern wonder not only disowns party allegiance, but repudiates any bias for class interests, aspiring to the nobler and more difficult mission of defending the good of all against the encroachments of any. It discusses not only the interests of classes and individuals with magisterial authority, but it presumes to pronounce on the conduct of governments, and even to arbitrate on the conflicting claims of nations. Truly, my Lord, this is a phenomenon which cannot but excite in almost an equal degree curiosity and interest, not unmingled with apprehension. This new power stands alone in Europe. To England belongs the distinction of its origin.

In fact. a journal like the London *Times* would be impossible anywhere else, for in no country does the public good at this day take such marked precedence over all other interests. The *Times* by a rare felicity has become the acknowledged champion of the national cause both at home and abroad, and it brings to its high task a depth of erudition, a grace and vigor of style, and, beyond all, a sagacious comprehension of English interests to be found only in the writings of a Burke, or the speeches of a Gladstone. It is a proud position for any journal to occupy, but a responsible one, and the *Times* gives it due heed. There are influences in England, dear to the nation, that watch it jealously. A mistake in judgment, or a partiality for private interests, would be fatal to its ascendency. Before pronouncing on a great question, domestic or foreign, the *Times* weighs anxiously its bearings on the national welfare, and then speaks with boldness and authority. In circulation it is outstripped by many obscure journals, but its moral power is unquestioned. Nor does it neglect any means of influence, for its information on every subject, from every quarter of the globe, surpasses in accuracy and celerity every other channel. An organ of opinion like this is a blessing to any country; for while it checks the aberrations of government, it removes from its path those cunning obstructions so often devised by the ambition of unprincipled men.

It may appear presumptuous to your Lordship that I should touch on so familiar a theme as the English Press, but it may not be without interest to see in what light it is regarded by a foreigner.

Our Press, as I have said, offers few points of resemblance to the French or English. A sprightly French writer has described it as not an *apostolat* so much as a *comptoir;* as less a *tribune* than an *affiche.* In other words, that its vocation is not to preach, but to assist trade; that it is not a pedestal for orators, but a place for advertisements. This is in some measure true. The prime mission of this country is the development of trade and commerce, and the Press derives its chief support from ministering to this universal thirst for acquisition.

The best criterion of the popularity of a journal in this country is the number of its advertisements; and to preserve them. it must regulate its course by the interests of the business community. All other considerations are subordinate. For this reason it may be perceived that our Press is perhaps less independent than that of England or France; for in the former its revenue is derived chiefly from circulation, the price being more remunerative than with us, while in the latter country it is sustained by party or government patronage; and consequently, an English or French journal, apart from the particular interest it advocates, is free and bold in its opinions. Again: I have no hesitation in saying that our Press has less influence over the public mind than in England or France; first, because it is not called upon to defend those conflicting political principles which grow out of the contention in Europe between royal prerogative and popular privilege, but chiefly because all classes with us are generally better instructed, and certainly more independent in mind and character; consequently our Press rarely seeks to guide, still less to dictate to public opinion. It is a far easier and safer rôle to follow in the beaten track of party lines, or to indorse on general subjects the expression of popular opinion.

It is a conclusive proof of the prevalence of Anti-slavery sentiment at the North at the present time, that the vast majority of the journals of this section are found in the ranks of the " Republicans." It may well be doubted if the convictions of all our public writers coincide with the opinions they deem it expedient to express, but it is an incontestable sign of the dominant pressure of the public mind in this country, that our Northern Press should so universally echo the views most acceptable in this latitude. There is but one journal at this ominous crisis that has courageously ventured to speak in the solemn voice of warning to the North, and to remind it that in yielding to a sentiment, or in gratifying an ambition, it runs the fearful risk of sacrificing its most solid interests. All honor is due to the *New York Herald* for its manly, judicious, and patriotic course. It has rightly understood that its allegiance to the great commercial community it represents, is best maintained by urging on the North, with incomparable tact and ability, to obey its judgment, and not abandon itself to impulse, —to make those just concessions which the occasion as well as duty demand.   It is a bold and perilous act in a journalist, at a moment when sectional feeling runs mountain high, to appeal, even in whispers, to the " still, small voice" of reason ; but the *Herald* has not shrunk from its self-imposed task.   Before the election of November, and since, it has not failed for a single day to beat the alarm-drum, and announce to its multitudinous readers that the country was in danger.   Identified with no party, shackled by no influence, it has no interest but the prosperity of our flourishing metropolis, and can have no object but the supreme good of our common country.   Can it be that all its efforts are vain, and that its valiant struggles to perpetuate the Union of these States cannot retard the decree which dooms them to dismemberment !   How many will deplore this grave calamity !   How many will exclaim hereafter

> " This might have been prevented, and made whole
> With very easy Arguments of Love !"

But should it be so ordained, then, there is not a lover of this country, not a friend of humanity, but will join in the eloquent and touching invocation your Lordship so recently uttered— " Whether that Union is destined to remain unimpaired, or whether those States are determined to separate into different communities, our present prayer is that the result may be brought about by amicable means.   Be it for maintaining the Union, or be it for dissolving the Union, may the world be spared the afflicting spectacle of a hostile conflict between brothers and brothers."*

* Extract from Lord Palmerston's speech at Southampton, January 8, 1861.

www.ingramcontent.com/pod-product-compliance
Lightning Source LLC
Chambersburg PA
CBHW021424090426
42742CB00009B/1247